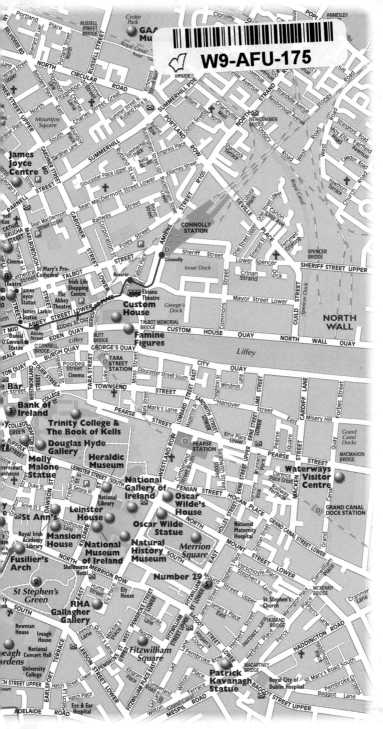

Dublin's
25Best

by Dr. Peter Harbison and Melanie Morris

Fodor's Travel Publications
New York • Toronto •
London • Sydney • Auckland
www.fodors.com

How to Use This Book

KEY TO SYMBOLS

✚ Map reference to the accompanying fold-out map

✉ Address

☎ Telephone number

🕐 Opening/closing times

🍴 Restaurant or café

🚆 Nearest rail station

Ⓜ Nearest subway (Metro) station

🚌 Nearest bus route

⛴ Nearest riverboat or ferry stop

♿ Facilities for visitors with disabilities

❓ Other practical information

▷ Further information

ℹ Tourist information

✋ Admission charges: Expensive (over €6), Moderate (€3–6), and Inexpensive (€3 or less)

★ Major Sight   ★ Minor Sight

👣 Walks   🔄 Excursions

🎁 Shops

🎭 Entertainment and Nightlife

🍴 Restaurants

This guide is divided into four sections

• **Essential Dublin:** an introduction to the city and tips on making the most of your stay.
• **Dublin by Area:** We've broken the city into four areas, and recommended the best sights, shops, entertainment venues, nightlife and restaurants in each one. Suggested walks help you to explore on foot.
• **Where to Stay:** the best hotels, whether you're looking for luxury, budget or something in between.
• **Need to Know:** the info you need to make your trip run smoothly, including getting about by public transport, weather tips, emergency phone numbers and useful websites.

Navigation In the Dublin by Area chapter, we've given each area of the city its own colour, which is also used on the locator maps throughout the book and the map on the inside front cover.

Maps The fold-out map accompanying this book is a comprehensive street plan of Dublin. The grid on this fold-out map is the same as the grid on the locator maps within the book. We've given grid references within the book for each sight and listing.

Contents

Introducing Dublin

Although The Celtic Tiger, as the Irish economy was nicknamed in the 1990s, has now been tamed and the buoyant mood has tempered, building and renovation in Dublin continues apace. The culture remains buzzing, youthful and cosmopolitan.

With the economic boom came an influx of artists, musicians, filmmakers, chefs and designers attracted by tax concessions and inexpensive property. Now the problem the country faces is that its success has made it the second most expensive country in Europe after Finland. The average house price in the city at the end of 2005 had risen to a whopping €468,273. The traffic is another problem being addressed and it is hoped that the Luas light rail system and the new Port Tunnel will ease congestion.

So how do Dubliners perceive their city? Many Dubs, as they are known, prospered on the strength of the service and IT industries. They have bought homes in smart leafy suburbs and commute to work, drink in wine bars, eat in the stylish restaurants and live the life of the new Dublin. Others maintain that the renovated Temple Bar is too 'gentrified' and that the development so loved by visitors and many young Dubliners has ruined the place. Fortunately Dublin does retain much of its intimacy and traditional Irish music and dance thrive. The old city is still there, especially beyond Grafton Street and Temple Bar where you can stroll in the squares and parks, visit old pubs or wander by a canal to find real Dubliners going about their daily lives. The population still cheers heartily for winning Gaelic football and hurling teams.

The schemes to develop the more run-down parts of the city are not just for tourists. The area north of the Liffey reaching to Collins Barracks in the west and O'Connell Street in the east—including Smithfield—and the huge development in Docklands is for residential housing as well as shops, offices, hotels, eating and cultural venues.

Facts + Figures

THE CHIMNEY IN SMITHFIELD

● This landmark has a 360° panorama of the city.

● Built in 1895 as a distillery chimney, it now has a two-tiered glass platform at a height of 56m (185ft).

● It is accessible via a glass elevator.

CRAIC

Craic (pronounced 'crack') is a word that describes fun, laughter and an overall good time. In Ireland people, places and events can all be 'great *craic*'. Pubs are *the* place for the *craic*, not just for drinking; they are where people join together for music, singing and talking. Even though the city is fast developing the pub remains the heart of its social life.

NICKNAMES

It is a tradition in Dublin to have nick-names for the numerous statues and monuments dotted around the city. For example spot the following:

● The Flue with the View
● The Hags with the Bags
● The Tart with the Cart
● The North Pole
● The Crank on the Bank
● Tone-henge

FASHIONABLE DISTRICT

Dignitaries and celebrities often stay 10 minutes from central Dublin, on the southeast side of the city. The fashion-able area of Ballsbridge and Lansdowne Road is near the interna-tional rugby ground (closed for reno-vation until 2008), the Royal Dublin Society's showgrounds and the exclu-sive embassy belt with its excellent restaurants and classy hotels.

A Short Stay in Dublin

DAY 1

Morning It wouldn't be a true trip to Ireland without acquainting yourself with the 'black stuff' and an early start at the **Guinness Storehouse** (▷ 30–31) will help you beat the crowds. You can get a bus down to St. James's Gate and spend a couple of hours touring the displays.

Mid-morning Take your free glass of Guinness and maybe a coffee at the Gravity Bar at the top of the Storehouse and you will be rewarded with some of the best views of the city. Catch a bus or walk back to view **Christ Church Cathedral** (▷ 26), and a trip around the adjoining **Dvblinia** (▷ 27) will give you an excellent insight into the medieval life of the city.

Lunch Walk from the Cathedral down Lord Edward Street into Dame Street. Just opposite **Dublin Castle** (▷ 28–29) you will find a quaint little tea shop the **Queen of Tarts** (▷ 44) where you can get an excellent light lunch. After lunch you may wish to visit the castle and the **Chester Beatty Library** (▷ 25), a rare and priceless book and Oriental art collection.

Afternoon Continue to the bottom of Dame Street taking a left turn into Anglesea Street. Carry on until you come to the quay and take a left and go first right over the Ha'Penny Bridge for good views of the River Liffey. Over the river cross two roads and you will come to the **shopping malls** (▷ 57) of Abbey Street and Henry Street. To the right you can follow through to **O'Connell Street** (▷ 52–53).

Dinner Return over the Ha'Penny Bridge and go straight into **Temple Bar** (▷ 34) with its choice of cosmopolitan restaurants, bars and pubs.

Evening Soak up the atmosphere of Temple Bar and take in a traditional Irish music session at **Oliver St. John Gogarty.** (▷ 40).

DAY 2

Morning The Book of Kells in **Trinity College** (▷ 72–73) is one of the most visited sights in Dublin and it is best to view as early as you can; the library opens at 9.30.

Mid-morning Walk round the front of the college and into Dublin's premier shopping street, Grafton Street, with its high-street names and designer shops. Stop for a coffee at the famous **Bewley's Oriental Café** (▷ 85). At the bottom of Grafton Street you will come to the **St. Stephen's Green Centre** (▷ 81), with **St. Stephen's Green** (▷ 70–71) to the left.

Lunch If the weather is nice have a picnic in the park or grab a bite to eat at the mall; try **Wagamama** (▷ 88) for something different.

Afternoon Take a stroll round the green, then take the exit to the north and cross over to Kildare Street. This is where you will find the grandest buildings in the city and fine museums, including the **National Museum** (▷ 66–67). Continue round to **Merrion Square** (▷ 75) with its wonderful reclining statue of **Oscar Wilde** (▷ 75). If quirky old-fashioned museums are your thing don't miss the **Natural History Museum** (▷ 68) when you continue down Merrion Street.

Dinner This is the locality of many of Dublin's top restaurants. Treat yourself at **Restaurant Patrick Guilbaud** (▷ 88) in the **Merrion Hotel** (▷ 112) Upper Merrion Street or **Lanyons** (▷ 87) in the Davenport Hotel Merrion Square, but expect to pay a price.

Evening You can choose here from traditional pubs or smooth classy bars—the city is at your feet.

▶ ▶ ▶

Bank of Ireland ▷ 24 One of Dublin's grandest and most impressive Palladian buildings.

Trinity College ▷ 72–73 Ireland's premier seat of learning houses perhaps the most beautiful book in the world.

Temple Bar ▷ 34 With its bohemian reputation and buzzing nightlife you won't get a quiet pint here.

St. Stephen's Green ▷ 70–71 Take a quiet break in this pleasant green space in the heart of Georgian Dublin.

St. Patrick's Cathedral ▷ 33 An embodiment of the history and heritage of the Irish people.

O'Connell Street ▷ 52–53 The revamped throughfare reflects poignant moments in the city's history.

Number Twenty Nine ▷ 69 A gem of Georgian architecture displaying typical 18th-century middle-class life.

Natural History Museum ▷ 68 Step back in time to view the wonderful Victorian stuffed animals and skeletons.

Casino, Marino ▷ 92 Captivating little villa in the suburb of Marino.

Chester Beatty Library ▷ 25 A most impressive library of Oriental and religious objects.

National Museum ▷ 66–67 Come here to see some great national treasures.

National Gallery ▷ 65 Ireland's foremost collection of art pays homage to the old masters.

These pages are a quick guide to the Top 25, which are described in more detail later. Here they are listed alphabetically and the tinted background shows the area they are in.

Christ Church Cathedral ▷ 26 The seat of Irish bishops since the time of Viking Dublin.

Collins Barracks ▷ 48 An impressive building housing a dazzling national art collection.

Dublin Castle ▷ 28–29 The hub of historic Dublin and seat and symbol of secular power. ▼▼▼

Dublin City Gallery The Hugh Lane ▷ 50 A gallery of Irish artists among a host of well-known painters.

Dublin Writers Museum ▷ 50 A glowing tribute to the great literary figures of the city.

Dvblinia ▷ 27 Relive life in medieval Dublin with this state-of-the art exhibition.

Glasnevin ▷ 93 Ireland's largest graveyard is the resting place for more than one million people.

Guinness Storehouse ▷ 30–31 The eponymous 'black stuff' venerated in this high-tech modern museum.

Heraldic Museum ▷ 64 Get back to your roots at this fascinating museum.

Irish Museum of Modern Art ▷ 96 Internationally acclaimed artists alongside up and coming local names.

James Joyce Centre ▷ 51 A cultural attraction devoted to the great man of Irish literature. ◀◀◀

DRUMCONDRA

Griffith Park

The Casino, Marino

Tolka Park

MARINO

Tolka

Royal Canal

PHIBSBOROUGH

Croke Park

Fairview Park

EAST WALL

Dublin Writers Museum

James Joyce Centre

Dublin City Gallery The Hugh Lane

O'Connell Street

NORTH WALL

Liffey

Temple Bar

Bank of Ireland

Trinity College & The Book of Kells

RINGSEND

Dublin Castle

Heraldic Museum

Chester Beatty Library

National Museum of Ireland

National Gallery of Ireland

Dodder

Marsh's Library

St Stephen's Green

Natural History Museum

Merrion Square

Number 29

Iveagh Gardens

Fitzwilliam Square

SOUTHEAST 61-88

RANELAGH

Grand Canal

BALLSBRIDGE

Marsh's Library ▷ 32 An impressive collection is housed in Ireland's first public library.

Kilmainham Gaol ▷ 94–95 Atmospheric and moving insight into profound moments of Irish history.

Shopping

The delight of shopping in bustling Dublin lies in the compact nature of the city and the proximity of the best shopping areas to one another. Major fashion houses are represented as are traditional, second-hand and retro shops.

Changing Tastes

Ireland's capital is becoming increasingly fashionable with its new found prosperity. Where before it was epitomized by its Celtic kitsch souvenirs—albeit still readily available—there is now a wealth of burgeoning home-grown talent. Craftspeople are merging the traditional with the modern. They continue to work in wood, silver, linen and wool but give the design a modern twist. What really makes shopping in Dublin is the variety and mix of shops available. You can still find shops selling only clothes for a child's first communion but now you also have the best in beautifully made items, trendy home interiors and top-quality Irish food products.

Shopping Areas

Generally, the best department stores and a wider variety of shops are north of the river on O'Connell Street and Henry Street. This busy area has been given a facelift and with the introduction of the new Luas tram service linking it with the up-and-coming Smithfield Village, it is now rivalling Grafton Street. Located south of the river, Grafton Street has always been

KNOW YOUR *BODHRÁN* FROM YOUR BANJO

The *bodhrán* (pronounced 'bough-rawn') is a simple and very old type of frame drum made of wood with animal skin—usually goat—stretched over the frame and beautifully decorated. It is played with a double-ended stick unlike most others, which are struck with the hands. Played for centuries in Ireland it came on to the world stage in the 1960s with the rise of the Irish band The Chieftains. If you can't master the technique, try hanging it on your wall!

Brown's store (top).
Fashionable Grafton Street
(middle). Crown Alley,
Temple Bar (bottom)

considered the smartest shopping area of the city and it remains popular with its main street chainstores, jewellery stalls, flower sellers, street musicians and a fine selection of the international and Irish fashion designer shops.

Irish Products

Sample bohemian South Great Georges Street, filled with second-hand clothes and ethnic stores. Busy Temple Bar's cobbled, winding streets have some craft design outlets. Dublin's antiques quarter, Francis Street, has beautiful furniture, Irish silver and wonderful one-of-a-kind pieces. For Irish crafts look for Aran knitwear—every sweater is unique. A Donegal tweed cap or hat makes a good souvenir. Jewellery has a special place in Dublin; look for the exquisite replicas of the Tara Brooch, Claddagh rings and Celtic knots mixing modern design with tradition. Waterford Crystal now uses designer John Rocha to produce clean, minimalist styles. Belleek is famous for its distinctive basket-weave pottery—and don't forget the delicate Irish linen and lace.

Traditional Buys

In home interior shops you'll find modern designs based on traditional patterns—visit Cow's Lane near Temple Bar. Dublin is the place to buy traditional musical instruments. And although much is mass produced in the Far East, Celtic kitsch is still part of Irish culture. Leprechauns, shamrocks and shillelaghs are in profusion.

LOCAL DELICACIES

Breads, farmhouse cheeses and salmon are a few of the local delights, along with handmade fresh cream chocolates and truffles. The Saturday market in Meeting House Square is a great place to buy these products. Look for Guinness-flavoured toffees and Irish Porter cake. The Old Jameson Distillery sells all manner of Irish whiskey flavoured items—truffles, jams, fudge, chutney—but don't forget a bottle of the real thing.

Temple Bar (top). Penny's store in Mary Street (middle). St. Stephen's Green mall (bottom)

Shopping by Theme

Whether you're looking for a department store, a quirky boutique, or something in between, you'll find it all in Dublin. On this page shops are listed by theme. For a more detailed write-up, see the individual listings in Dublin by Area.

Dublin by Night

Whether you like clubs, trendy cocktail bars or traditional pubs, there is no shortage of venues. Dublin's theatres are famous—play-wrights such as Brian Friel continue to garner accolades in London and New York—and feature a wide repertoire of plays and opera for the more cultural evening, or perhaps you prefer to catch one of the latest releases at the cinema.

Anyone for a Drink?

Dublin pubs are an institution and pub crawls make for a great night out, especially when you try to track down the thickest and tastiest pint of Guinness or Murphy's, or a lighter lager—Harp is brewed in Dublin. Although most pubs close at 11pm, 11.30pm or 12.30am, some pubs, bars and clubs serve alcohol late—until 2.30 on one or more nights. There is now a smoking ban in all pubs. Watch out for leaflets of Irish music or jazz and rock sessions in many pubs and bars.

Laughter or Dancing?

Expanding fast, Dublin's comedy scene sees lots of new talent emerging and comedy clubs seem to open all the time. There is stand-up comedy at many pubs every night; on open-mike nights comedians and other acts battle it out to be acclaimed as the night's best act. The Comedy Cellar on Wicklow Street still features international comedians such as Ardal O'Hanlon and Tommy Tiernan. Dance clubs, which have multiplied dramatically since the mid-1990s, pulse with hardcore, garage, techno and chart toppers.

Cheers in Irish is slainte. *Have a traditional night out in a pub or go to one of Dublin's historic theatres*

MERRION SQUARE

Evening light is kind to Dublin's Georgian architecture. Under illumination the imposing buildings and elegant squares resemble the set of a magnificent period drama. Take an evening stroll around Merrion Square, down Merrion Street Upper and on to Baggot Street to see the dramatic sight of the illuminated National Museums and the Government Buildings.

Eating Out

With the growth of tourism in Dublin new restaurants and bars are opening up at a bewildering speed and many of them are very good. Young, talented Irish chefs have transformed the menus and placed great emphasis on good-quality local ingredients. You really are spoiled for choice. Eating out is not cheap in Dublin but you can take advantage of 'early-bird' menus, served before 7pm or less-expensive lunchtime menus.

What's on Offer?
International cuisine has hit the city in recent years and has been enthusiastically embraced by innovative restaurateurs. Choose from Asian, including Thai, Indian and Chinese, a myriad of European restaurants or the less well-known, including Mexican and Lebanese.

Irish Cooking
Despite the upsurge of international cooking, Irish cuisine has had something of a renaissance. The concept of New Irish Cuisine has replaced the original rather heavy dishes, using cheaper ingredients, although some of the pubs do still serve the traditional fare. The basis of the recipes are the same but a modern interpretation is now the concept, producing lighter more acceptable food.

Mealtimes
Breakfast may be served anytime from 7am until 10am, depending on the establishment, with lunch from about 12 until 2 or 2.30pm. An increasing number of places stay open all day, and some pubs serve food all day. Dinner is served early, from about 6pm and might stop by 10pm, but you will find places open later, notably Indian and Chinese restaurants.

Dress Code
As with most things in life, the Irish take a very laid-back approach to dress codes. Casual attire is fine in all but the most expensive restaurants and some of the smarter hotel restaurants.

There is so much on offer in Dublin, from oyster bars to historic cafés to stylish and trendy eateries

Restaurants by Cuisine

There are restaurants to suit all tastes and budgets in Dublin. On this page they are listed by cuisine. For a more detailed description of each restaurant, see Dublin by Area.

CASUAL DINING

Bad Ass Café (▷ 42)
Cocoon (▷ 86)
Dockers (▷ 106)
Eddie Rockets (▷ 86)
FXB (▷ 42)
Gallaghers Boxty House (▷ 42)
Old Jameson Distillery (▷ 60)
Pasta Fresca (▷ 88)
The Shack (▷ 44)
Thomas Read (▷ 44)

COFFEE AND TEA

Avoca Cafés (▷ 106)
Bewley's Oriental Café (▷ 85)
BT2 (▷ 85)
Kaffe Mocka (▷ 87)
Queen of Tarts (▷ 44)
The Terrace Lounge (▷ 88)

ELEGANT DINING

Brownes Restaurant (▷ 85)
L'Ecrivain (▷ 86)
Fire (▷ 86)
Halo (▷ 60)
Lanyons (▷ 87)
Les Frères Jacques (▷ 43)
Longchamps @ No. 10 (▷ 87)
One Pico (▷ 88)
Restaurant Patrick Guilbaud (▷ 88)
The Tea Room at the Clarence (▷ 44)

INTERNATIONAL

Ar Vicoletto Osteria Romana (▷ 42)
Aya (▷ 85)
Il Baccaro (▷ 43)
Bahay Kubo (▷ 106)
Bella Cuba (▷ 106)
Botticelli (▷ 42)
The Cedar Tree (▷ 42)
Chili Club (▷ 86)
Diep Le Shaker (▷ 86)
Eastern Balti House (▷ 86)
Harbourmaster Bar & Restaurant (▷ 106)
Imperial (▷ 87)
Kelly & Ping (▷ 60)
Langkawi (▷ 87)
La Mère Zou (▷ 87)
Mexico to Rome (▷ 43)
Mongolian Barbeque (▷ 43)
Monty's of Katmandu (▷ 43)
Rajdoot Tandoori (▷ 88)
Shalimar (▷ 44)
Steps of Rome (▷ 88)
Tante Zoe's (▷ 44)
Thai Orchid (▷ 44)
Trastevere (▷ 44)
Ukiyo Bar (▷ 44)
Trentuno (▷ 88)
Wagamama (▷ 88)
Yamamori (▷ 44)

SNACKS

Alpha Restaurant (▷ 85)
Café Java (▷ 86)
Chompys (▷ 86)
Cobalt Café (▷ 60)
Elephant and Castle (▷ 42)
Expresso Bar (▷ 86)
Keoghs (▷ 87)
Lemon Crepe & Coffee Co. (▷ 43)
Nude (▷ 88)
Odessa Lounge & Grill (▷ 43)

TREND SETTERS

Bang Café (▷ 85)
Brasserie Na Mara (▷ 106)
Eden (▷ 42)
Fitzers (▷ 87)
Jacob's Ladder (▷ 87)
John M. Keating (▷ 60)
Mao (▷ 87)
Mermaid Café (▷ 43)

VEGETARIAN/FISH

Café Fresh (▷ 85)
Cavistons (▷ 106)
Cornucopia (▷ 86)
Guinea Pig (The Fish Restaurant) (▷ 106)
Juice (▷ 43)
King Sitric (▷ 106)
Leo Burdock's (▷ 43)
Lord Edward (▷ 43)
Ocean (▷ 88)

If You Like...

However you'd like to spend your time in Dublin, these top suggestions should help you tailor your ideal visit. Each sight or listing has a fuller write-up in Dublin by Area.

BEST IRISH BUYS

Brown Thomas department store (▷ 78) showcases established and up and coming Irish designers.
The Avoca (▷ 78) store is full of all things Irish and the food hall is brimming with tasty delights.
Waltons (▷ 33) is the place for your musical instruments Irish-style from *bodhráns* to whistles.

STYLE GURUS

All your designer accessories for the home can be bought at Haus (▷ 37), a contemporary interior heaven.
From kitchen to living room you should find something to suit you in Stock (▷ 81).
If it is fine art you are after go to former fashion designer Ib Jorgensen's gallery (▷ 79).

From traditonal to trendy— some new tastes while you are in Dublin and you won't be disappointed

EASTERN DELIGHTS

Eastern cooking with a nod to the west can be found in Smithfield at Kelly & Ping restaurant (▷ 60).
Try a sophisticated Thai eating experience at Diep Le Shaker (▷ 86).
Head for the popular Japanese restaurant Yamamori (▷ 44) for noodles and sushi.

FISHY BUSINESS

You'll get great waterside views and delicious fish at Ocean (▷ 88).
DART out to Howth for the freshest of fish at the expensive, but worth it, King Sitric restaurant (▷ 106).
Down to earth fish 'n' chips at their best from Leo Burdock's takeout (▷ 43).

ESSENTIAL DUBLIN IF YOU LIKE...

Elegant, fashionable but always maintaining the traditional in Dublin's fair city

STAYING AT A GEORGIAN TOWNHOUSE

Four townhouses in one, the Merrion (▷ 112) is one of Dublin's most luxurious hotels—period elegance at its best.
Savour Longfields (▷ 111), an intimate Georgian gem in Merrion Square, the perfect retreat.
Relax at Staunton's on the Green (▷ 111), close to the city centre, an oasis of calm with a garden.

FASHIONABLE NIGHTLIFE

Dress to impress at Lillie's Bordello (▷ 82) where celebs and the beautiful people hang out.
Pod (▷ 83) is a hip joint with a variety of sounds on different nights.
Opulence, big time, at the Café en Seine (▷ 82), a lively venue for cocktails and atmosphere.

TRADITIONAL MUSIC

Listen to Irish music every night upstairs at the Temple Bar pub, Oliver St. John Gogarty (▷ 40).
For impromptu music visit O'Donaghue's (▷ 83), one time haunt of The Dubliners.
For dancing as well as music try O'Shea's Merchant (▷ 41) and be prepared for audience participation.

The musical heritage of Ireland is alive and kicking in pubs all over Dublin

THINGS FOR KIDS

Dublin Zoo (▷ 97), provides plenty of cuddly and not so cuddly animals to view.
Start on the road and then take to the water with the Viking Splash company (▷ 35).
For scares, visit the Bram Stoker Dracula Experience (▷ 97), but you've been warned.

AN INEXPENSIVE TRIP

Stay in a hostel—try Kinlay House (▷ 109).
Eat a big, good value, breakfast at Alpha
Restaurant (▷ 85) to set you up for the day.
Stroll through the parks or
Georgian squares, such as Merrion
Square (▷ 75), it's free.

Getting away from city life is easy in Ireland's capital

LUXURY TO BE SURE

Be pampered at the Morrison
(▷ 112) with its new spa and
Turkish bath.
Dine at Ireland's leading French
restaurant, Patrick Guilbaud
(▷ 88).
Shop at Louise Kennedy
(▷ 80) in Merrion Square for
beautiful clothes and gifts.

THE GREAT OUTDOORS

Stroll in big Phoenix Park (▷ 98) or the less
well known peaceful Iveagh Gardens (▷ 74).
Take a trip on the DART (▷ 100–101) for a
breath of sea air.
Play a round of golf—the choice of courses is
huge (▷ 105).

LITERARY GREATS

Find out about them all at the Dublin Writers
Museum (▷ 50).
James Joyce is synonymous with Dublin, get all
the gen on the great man at the James Joyce
Centre (▷ 51).
Oscar Wilde reclines languidly on a rock in
Merrion Square, while his house
(▷ 75) is on the corner.
Visit the simple childhood home
of one of Dublin's famous literary
sons, George Bernard Shaw (▷ 35).

Green space is abundant in Dublin's gorgeous Georgian squares

*Turn back the clock to another century at the
home of the literary great, George Bernard
Shaw*

Dublin by Area

THE SOUTHWEST

THE NORTH

THE SOUTHEAST

FARTHER AFIELD

The Southwest

Although not the most attractive district of the city, the southwest area is one of the most historically interesting. From the early Celtic and Viking settlements the medieval walled city of Dublin developed.

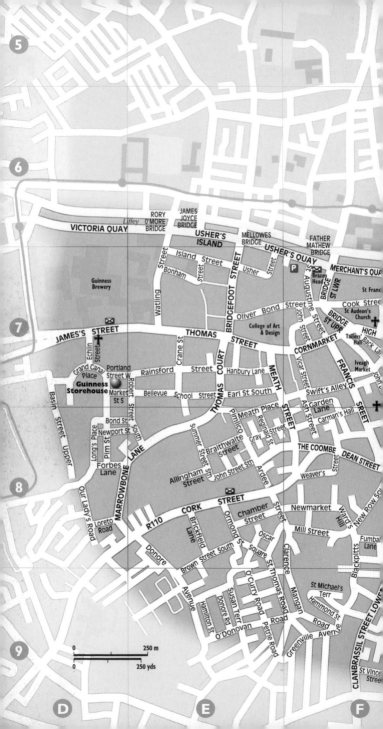

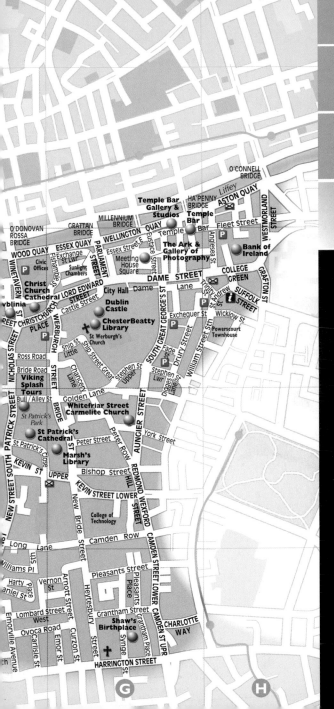

O'CONNELL BRIDGE

Liffey

ASTON QUAY

HA'PENNY BRIDGE

Temple Bar Gallery & Studios

Temple Bar

WESTMORLAND STREET

Fleet Street

Temple Bar

MILLENNIUM BRIDGE

WELLINGTON QUAY

Temple

GRATTAN BRIDGE

Essex Street E

The Ark & Gallery of Photography

Bank of Ireland

O'DONOVAN ROSSA BRIDGE

ESSEX QUAY

Exchange St LWR

Meeting House Square

Eustace Street

COLLEGE GREEN

GRAFTON ST

WOOD QUAY

Civic Offices

Fishamble St

Sunlight Chambers

PARLIAMENT STREET

DAME STREET

Dame Lane

St Andrew St

SUFFOLK ST

WINETAVERN ST

Christ Church Cathedral

LORD EDWARD STREET

City Hall

COLLEGE

Anglesea St

Wicklow St

bblinia

CHRISTCHURCH PLACE

Castle Street

Dublin Castle

Dame

SOUTH GREAT GEORGE'S ST

Exchequer St

Trinity St

Powerscourt Townhouse

REET

WERBURGH STREET

ChesterBeatty Library

St Werburgh's Church

Ship St Little

Fade St

Drury Street

William Street

Ross Road

Ship Street Great

Stephen St Upper

NICHOLAS STREET

Bride Road

Chancery Lane

Stephen St Lwr

Digges Lane

Viking Splash Tours

BRIDE STREET

Golden Lane

Bull / Alley St

St Patrick's Park

Whitefriar Street Carmelite Church

SOUTH PATRICK STREET

St Patrick's Close

St Patrick's Cathedral

Peter Street

Peter Row

York Street

AUNGIER STREET

NEW STREET SOUTH

Marsh's Library

Bishop Street

REDMOND HILL

KEVIN ST UPPER

KEVIN STREET LOWER

WEXFORD STREET

New Bride St

College of Technology

Long Lane

Luls

Camden Row

Williams PI

Harty Place

Vernon St

Pleasants Street

Pleasants Place

CAMDEN STREET LOWER

CAMDEN ST UPR

aniel St

Arnott Street

Heytesbury

Lombard Street West

Ovoca Road

Curzon St

Emor St

Grantham Street

Grantham Place

CHARLOTTE WAY

Emorville Avenue

Carlisle St

Shaw's Birthplace

Synge Street

HARRINGTON STREET

G

H

The Southwest

Bank of Ireland

TOP 25

Like a building from classical Greece, the Bank of Ireland also has stunning taspestries

THE BASICS

+ H7
- 2 College Green
- 677 6801
- House of Lords:
Mon–Fri 10–4, Wed
10.30–4, Thu 10–5
- Tara Street
- Cross-city buses
- Few
- Free
- Tours of House of Lords
Tue 10.30, 11.30, 1.45

HIGHLIGHTS

● Exterior detail
● Former House of Lords
with barrel-vaulted ceiling
● Jan van Beaver tapestries
● Crystal chandelier

This great semicircular building was the focus of Ireland's glorious years of freedom at the end of the 18th century, when the city reached the zenith of its architectural and artistic achievement.

Harmony The Bank of Ireland, overlooking College Green, began life as the upper and lower houses of the old Irish Parliament, which gained its legislative independence in 1782 but saw its members bribed to vote itself out of existence 18 years later. Its first architect was Edward Lovett Pearce, who designed the recessed south-facing 'piazza' of Ionic columns (c1729–39) and the rooms behind it, of which the old House of Lords is still intact and often accessible to the public. It has a striking barrel-vaulted ceiling, a splendid oak and marble fireplace and features a wonderful Dublin crystal chandelier (1788) of 1,233 pieces, and two fine tapestries (1733) by Jan van Beaver—one of King James II at the 1689 Siege of Londonderry, the other of King William of Orange at the 1690 Battle of the Boyne.

Alterations The architect James Gandon added the curving and windowless screen and the east-facing Corinthian portico between 1785 and 1789, and a corresponding portico was added to the west side some years later. After the parliament was dissolved, the building was sold in 1802 to the Bank of Ireland, on condition that it be modified to prevent it from being used again for public debate. This was done by Francis Johnston and included the present banking rooms.

Chester Beatty Library

Hidden away behind the ivy, the Chester Beatty Library reveals its Chinese ceiling

Sir Alfred Chester Beatty is one of the few people to have been made an honorary citizen of Ireland for bequeathing to the nation in 1956 such a rare and priceless art collection.

Hidden treasure The library and Oriental art gallery named after its founder and benefactor, Sir Alfred Chester Beatty (1875–1968), is one of Dublin's jewels but often overlooked. The priceless and unique collection is housed in a converted Georgian building.

Masterpieces Alfred Chester Beatty, a successful mining engineer born in New York and knighted for his services to Britain as an advisor to Winston Churchill during World War II, devoted an important part of his life to the search for manuscripts and *objets d'art* of the highest quality. The collections range from c2700BC up to the 19th century, and stretch geographically from Japan in the east to Europe in the west. Religious writings range from one of the earliest known New Testament papyri to the Korans, all masterpieces of calligraphy. There is a wealth of Persian and Mughal miniature paintings as well as wonders of the East such as Burmese and Siamese painted fairy-tale books or *parabaiks*, Chinese silk paintings and jade snuff bottles, and Japanese *netsuke* and woodblock prints. Exhibitions are focused on two diverse themes—Great Religions of the World and Secular Arts and Patronage. The library won the Gulbenkian Heritage Council Irish Museum of the Year Award in 2000.

THE BASICS

www.cbl.ie

➕ G7

✉ The Clock Tower Building, Dublin Castle

☎ 407 0750

🕐 Mon–Fri 10–5 (closed Mon Oct–end Apr), Sat 11–5, Sun 1–5

🍴 Café

🚇 Tara Street

🚌 Cross-city buses

♿ Good

💷 Free; charge for special events

❓ Audio-visual. Free guided tours

HIGHLIGHTS

- New Testament papyri
- Koran manuscripts
- Persian and Mughal paintings
- Jade snuff bottles

Christt Church Cathedral

The superb nave (far left) of Christ Church (middle). Treasures in the Crypt (right)

THE BASICS

www.cccdub.ie

F7

Christchurch Place

677 8099

Jun–end Aug daily 9–6; Sep–end May daily 9.45–5. Treasures: Mon–Fri 9.45–5, Sat 10–4.45, Sun 12.30–3.15

50, 51B, 78A, 123

Good

Requested donation €5; Treasures exhibition: moderate

HIGHLIGHTS

● 12th-century south transept
● Leaning north wall
● Knight's effigy
● Crypt and 'Treasures of Christ Church'

Christ Church Cathedral is not only Dublin's oldest stone building but also perhaps the Normans' outstanding contribution to Irish architecture. It reflects 1,000 years of worship in Ireland.

History The older of Dublin's two cathedrals, Christ Church was founded by the Norse king Sigtryggr Silkenbeard in 1038. The northern side of the choir and the south transept are the oldest parts of the existing stone structure and have been dated back to just before 1180, indicating that the Normans started the building shortly after they took over the city, using masons brought over from the west of England. The early Gothic nave, dated c1226–36, also reflects English influence. Its vault collapsed in 1562, leaving the north wall with an outward lean of about 51cm (20in).

Restoration The whole building would now be a romantic ivied ruin but for the intervention of the Dublin whiskey distiller Henry Roe, who paid for its reconstruction between 1872 and 1878. The work was carried out under the direction of the great English Victorian architect George Edmund Street, who added flying buttresses to keep the whole edifice standing. Look for the effigy of a knight in armour near the entrance, traditionally thought to represent the great Norman knight, Strongbow (Robert de Clare). An unusual feature is the original crypt, extending the entire length of the cathedral and housing the 'Treasures of Christ Church' exhibition, which features a video of the cathedral's history.

Dvblinia and the Viking World

Learn about life in medieval Dublin and meet the Vikings—but mind the stocks

If you want to know just what made Dublin's medieval ancestors tick, check out the Dvblinia exhibition, a scale model of the medieval city with tableaux and an audio-visual show.

Vivid re-creation Dvblinia, as the town was first recorded on a map *c*1540, is a vibrant re-creation of medieval Dublin life housed in the Victorian-era former Synod Hall. After the Vikings had reestablished the city in this area during the 10th century, Hiberno-Norsemen and Normans occupied it from 1170 until the end of the Middle Ages—the time-span covered by Dvblinia. The newest exhibition 'The Viking World' reveals a fascinating glimpse of the Viking past.

Excavations One of the most impressive features is the scale model that shows Dublin as it was around 1500; Christ Church Cathedral is inside the city walls and St. Patrick's Cathedral beyond. Thirty years of excavations in the Dvblinia area have uncovered many fascinating objects such as leatherwork, pottery decorated with amusing faces, floor tiles, jewellery and ships' timbers, which are also on view in the exhibition. An audio-visual presentation of the city's history complements the series of life-size model tableaux that illustrate episodes from the past. Climb the 96 steps inside the tower of 15th-century St. Michael's Church, incorporated into the Synod Hall when it was built, for great views of the city and the river. Dvblinia was voted Best Smaller Museum in the Museum of the Year Award, 2001.

THE BASICS

www.dublinia.ie
✚ F7
✉ St. Michael's Hill, Christchurch
☎ 679 4611
🕐 Apr–end Sep daily 10–5; Oct–end Mar Mon–Sat 11–4 (Sun and public hols) 10–4.30
🚌 50, 51B, 123
🍴 Café
♿ Dvblinia: good. Tower and bridge: none
💷 Moderate
❓ Prebookable tours

HIGHLIGHTS

● Re-creation of medieval Dublin
● Scale model
● Interactive re-created Medieval Fair
● Medieval objects
● View over Dublin

THE SOUTHWEST ★ TOP 25

Dublin Castle

- Powder Tower
- State Apartments
- Chapel Room

How many buildings in Europe can claim to have been the hub of a country's secular power for longer than Dublin Castle, the headquarters of English rule in Ireland for more than 700 years?

Ancient site Dublin Castle, now used for State occasions, presidential inaugurations and occasional European summit meetings, stands on the site of a much older Viking settlement. It occupies the southeastern corner of the Norman walled town overlooking the long-vanished black pool or *dubh linn* that gave the city its ancient Irish name. The castle's defined rectangular shape was determined from the start in 1204 with the construction of a twin-towered entrance on the north side and stout circular bastions at each corner. The excavated remains of one of these, the Powder

The red drawing room at Dublin Castle (far left). The elegant throne room (left). The façade of the castle has seen many alterations over the centries (right). A depiction of the Great Courtyard dating from 1792 (below left). A ceiling painting in St. Patrick's Hall (below middle). A fountain in the castle grounds (below right)

Tower, shown on the guided tour, rested on an earlier Viking foundation and was attached to the city wall beside an arch, beneath which water flowed from the old castle moat.

Interior After a fire in 1684, the interior was almost entirely rebuilt in the 18th and early 19th centuries. On the south side of Upper Castle Yard are the State Apartments, where the English king's viceroy lived until the castle was handed over to the Irish State in 1922. These regal rooms form the second half of the guided tour, which starts in the Powder Tower.

City Hall Next door to the castle is the imposing City Hall with its interesting exhibition, The Story of Capital (Mon–Sat 10–5.15, Sun 2–5). Check out the fabulous celings in the entrance hall.

THE BASICS

www.dublincastle.ie

✚ G7

✉ Dame Street

☎ 677 7129

🕐 Mon–Fri 10–5, Sat, Sun, and public hols 2–5. State Apartments closed occasionally for functions

🍽 Restaurant

🚉 Tara Street

🚌 Cross-city buses

♿ State Apartments: good. Powder Tower: none

💷 Moderate

❓ Gardens, open Mon–Fri, do not form part of tour

Guinness Storehouse

Think Dublin, think Guinness. An integral part of the city's economy and history, the 'black stuff' is known throughout the world. The Guinness Experience should not be missed.

What's in a glass? As you enter the 1904 building through a stone arch an escalator takes you up into the middle of the building. You then walk into what is described as a large pint glass. Within this glass structure your journey through the production process of a pint of Guinness begins. Simple, dramatic displays show the four basic ingredients, hops, barley, yeast and water, all of which you can touch, feel and smell. The displays provoke the senses as indicated on the huge wall label reading 'Smells are delectable too, the heavy sleepy scent of hops—steam hot metal, sweat'.

*Take a drink in the Gravity Bar offering one of the finest views of Dublin (left)
The Guinnness Storehouse illuminated at night—an icon of Dublin's economy, past and present (right)*

Mine's a pint You follow the pint as it makes its way through the brewery of the past founded by Arthur Guinness in 1759—a past still much in evidence today. Old machinery is cleverly utilized, doubling up as interactives to give you more information. From the brewing process you go to the transportation section, with large-scale models showing how Guinness has reached the far-flung corners of the world. The advertising display is great fun, with popular memorabilia and a hall of fame recalling classic Guinness advertisements. Finally, you learn how Guinness has affected many aspects of Irish life as supporter of the arts, festivals and sport. You finish your journey at the top of the glass, in the Gravity bar, with a splendid view over Dublin and your free pint. In September 2005, the Storehouse welcomed its 3 millionth visitor since opening in December 2000.

THE BASICS

www.guinness-storehouse.com

✚ D7

✉ St. James's Gate

☎ 404 4800

🕐 Daily 9.30–5, (until 8 in Jul, Aug)

🍴 Brewery Bar, Gravity Bar, Source Restaurant

🚌 51B, 78A from Aston Quay; 123 from O'Connell Street

♿ Excellent

💷 Expensive

❓ Shop

Marsh's Library

The oldest public library in Ireland is light years away from modern Dublin

THE BASICS

www.marshlibrary.ie
✚ G8
✉ St. Patrick's Close
☎ 454 3511
🕐 Mon, Wed, Thu, Fri 10–1, 2–5, Sat 10.30–1
🚌 Cross-city buses
♿ Few
💷 Inexpensive

HIGHLIGHTS

● Old-world atmosphere
● Oak bookcases
● 'Cages' for rare works
● Books and manuscripts

This magnificent example of an 18th-century scholar's library has changed little since it opened nearly 300 years ago. One of the few buildings here to retain its original purpose, it remains a calm oasis of scholarly learning.

Rare legacy In 1701, Archbishop Narcissus Marsh (1638–1713) built Ireland's first public library close to St. Patrick's Cathedral and filled it with his own books and 10,000 others purchased in 1705 from the Bishop of Worcester. Two years later, it was given official legal standing when the Irish parliament passed an Act for 'settling and preserving a public library'. The building is one of the city's rare legacies from the reign of Queen Anne and was designed by Sir William Robinson, responsible for the Royal Hospital at Kilmainham (▷ 94–95), using distinctive grey Dublin limestone on one side and red brick on the front.

Precious books Inside, the long gallery is flanked on each side by dark oak bookcases adorned with carved and lettered gables topped by carvings of an archbishop's mitre. At the end of the L-shape gallery are three alcoves or 'cages', where readers were locked with the library's precious books. As an extra safeguard, chains were attached to the books (though not to the readers). The volumes reflect the founder's wide-ranging interests, and the oldest example is Cicero's Letters to his Friends, published in Milan in 1472. The library also possesses some 300 manuscripts, displayed with other items in glass-fronted cases.

St. Patrick's Cathedral

'Here is laid the body of Jonathan Swift, Doctor of Divinity, Dean of this Cathedral Church, where fierce indignation can no longer rend the heart. Go traveller, and imitate, if you can, this earnest and dedicated champion of liberty.'

Literary connections Jonathan Swift's epitaph is a fitting tribute to the personality most often associated with St. Patrick's Cathedral. The author of *Gulliver's Travels*—written as a political satire but enjoyed by generations of children—Swift was the cathedral's fearless and outspoken Dean from 1713 until his death in 1745. He and his beloved Stella, rumoured to have been his wife, are buried inside the modern entrance.

History Founded as a church in 1192, and raised to cathedral status in 1219, St. Patrick's was built in the early English Gothic style and completed by 1284. The fact that Dublin has two Protestant cathedrals is something of a paradox in a predominantly Catholic city and country. Like Christ Church (▷ 26), St. Patrick's was heavily restored in the 19th century, entirely with funds from the wealthy Guinness family.

Monuments Look for the tomb and effigy of the 17th-century adventurer Richard Boyle, Earl of Cork, and a memorial to the great Irish bard and harpist Turlough O' Carolan (1670–1738). In the south choir aisle are two of Ireland's rare 16th-century monumental brasses. The cathedral organ is the largest in Ireland.

THE BASICS

www.stpatrickscathedral.ie
+ F8
✉ St. Patrick's Street
☎ 453 9472
🕐 Mar–end Oct Mon–Sat 9–5.15, Sun 9–10.30, 12.30–2.30, 4.15–6; Nov–end Feb Mon–Sat 9–5, Sun 10–11, 12.45–3
🚌 Cross-city buses
♿ Good
💶 Moderate
ℹ Living Stones exhibition explores St. Patrick's history

HIGHLIGHTS

● Swift's bust and epitaph
● Medieval brasses
● Memorial to O'Carolan
● Organ
● Living Stones Exhibition

Temple Bar

The bright shops of Crown Alley in Temple Bar (left). Advertising the 'black stuff' (right)

THE BASICS

www.templebar.ie

➕ G7

✉ Temple Bar Information Centre, 12 East Essex Street, Temple Bar

☎ 677 22551

🚉 Tara Street 🚌 Cross-city buses

Meeting House Square

➕ G7

✉ Temple Bar

🚉 Tara Street 🚌 Cross-city buses

HIGHLIGHTS

● Meeting House Square
● Pubs, bars and cafés
● Shops in Cow's Lane
● Street theatre

The area known as Temple Bar lies between Dame Street and the River Liffey and covers some 11ha (27 acres). It takes its name from the Anglo-Irish aristocrat, Sir William Temple, who owned land here in the 17th century.

Early beginnings Business flourished in Temple Bar from the early 17th century but the area fell into decline in the early 20th century and by the late 1980s had been proposed as the site for a new bus terminal. Objections were vociferous and the city's 'left bank' began to take off.

Dublin's Cultural Quarter Today, pedestrian-friendly and with restricted vehicle access, this is a vibrant cultural district and the main draw for tourists with its mix of restaurants, shops, pubs and bars. It is the venue for the Gallery of Photography, the Ark and the Temple Bar Gallery and Studios (▷ opposite page). Temple Bar has almost been too successful for its own good and as its popularity has grown so have the crowds and at times unwanted unruly behaviour. It does still get rowdy at weekends, but during the day and on weekday nights it is great fun to be in. Development continues with the renewal of Cow's Lane, Dublin's oldest district.

Meeting House Square In the heart of Temple Bar this square is the focus for performance art, the summer open-air cinema and the wonderful Saturday market (▷ panel 38). This is a showcase for Irish talent be it art, music or juggling.

THE ARK

www.theark.ie

This specially created cultural venue for children 4–14 years offers around 10 events a year on art and culture.

➕ G7 ✉ 11a Eustace Street ☎ 670 7788
🚉 Tara Street 🚌 Cross-city buses
♿ Good 🕐 Depends on activity

GALLERY OF PHOTOGRAPHY

Ireland's leading hub for contemporary photography.

➕ G7 ✉ Meeting House Square
☎ 671 4654 🕐 Tue–Sat 11–6, Sun 1–6

SHAW BIRTHPLACE

The childhood home of playwright George Bernard Shaw (1856–1950) is full of Victorian charm.

➕ G9 ✉ 33 Synge Street ☎ 475 0854
🕐 May–end Sep Mon, Tue, Thu, Fri 10–5, Sat, Sun and public hols 2–5. Closed for tours 1–2 🚌 16, 16A, 19 ♿ Few 🕐 Expensive

TEMPLE BAR GALLERY & STUDIOS

Exhibition space on three floors and 30 artists' studios. Contemporary art from established and emerging artists.

➕ G6 ✉ 5–9 Temple Bar ☎ 671 0073
🕐 Tue–Sat 11–6 (until 7 Thu) 🚉 Tara Street 🚌 Cross-city buses

VIKING SPLASH TOURS

www.vikingsplashtours.com

Passengers are driven through Viking Dublin on amphibious buses before driving into the Grand Canal to finish the tour on water. Fun and educational.

➕ F8 ✉ 64–65 Patrick Street (office)
☎ 707 6000 🕐 Regular daily tours depart from Bull Alley and St. Stephen's Green, check as times can vary 🕐 Expensive

WHITEFRIAR STREET CARMELITE CHURCH

Whitefriars is administered by the Carmelite order who reestablished the church here in 1827. The church contains the relics of the patron saint of lovers, St. Valentine.

➕ G8 ✉ 56 Aungier Street ☎ 475 8821
🕐 Mon, Wed–Fri 7.45am–6pm, Tue 7.45am–9.15pm, Sat–Sun 7.45am–7.30pm
🚉 Pearse 🚌 Cross-city buses ♿ Good
🕐 Free

The music room in Shaw's Birthplace

Shrine in Whitefriar Street Carmelite Church

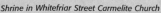

Walk Along the Quays

The English-born architect James Gandon (1743–1823) played an important role in the beautification of Dublin.

DISTANCE: 1.5km (1mile) **ALLOW:** 45 minutes

START

GEORGE'S QUAY
➕ J6 🚌 Cross-city buses

1 Start at George's Quay and look across to the Custom House (▷ 54), a magnificent neo-classical building, built by James Gandon between 1781 and 1789.

2 At O'Connell Bridge, glance left along Westmoreland Street to see the portico (c1784–89), that Gandon added to the Old Parliament House, now the Bank of Ireland (▷ 24).

3 Continue upstream past the metal bridge, known as the Ha'Penny Bridge, constructed in 1816. Carry on past the pedestrian Millennium Bridge.

4 At the Grattan Bridge look south along Parliament Street to Thomas Cooley's imposing City Hall (▷ 29), the headquarters of Dublin Corporation since 1852.

END

FOUR COURTS (▷ 54)
➕ F6 🚌 Cross-city buses

8 Here you will have the best view over the river of Gandon's second masterpiece the Four Courts (▷ 54) built between 1786 and 1802.

7 Continue past the Civic offices on your left, where excavations unearthed a Viking site in the 1970s until you reach Merchant's Quay. This was the site of the first Viking crossing of the River Liffey when they arrived in Dublin back in the 9th century.

6 While still by the Grattan Bridge have a look at the striking seahorse statues. Just beyond is Betty Maguire's Viking Boat scultpure (20th century) outside the Civic Offices.

5 It was built in 1769, some time before Gandon arrived in Dublin.

Shopping

CLADDAGH RECORDS
www.claddaghrecords.com
Specialist music shop hidden away in a Temple Bar backstreet. It sells CDs and tapes from the countryfied sound of Irish dance bands to the archly traditional and contemporary. The staff know their stuff.
🕂 G7 ✉ 2 Cecilia Street, Temple Lane ☎ 677 0262 🚊 Tara Street 🚌 Cross-city buses

COW'S LANE MARKET
This is a fashion and design market that specializes in handmade, one off Irish design in clothing, housewares and jewellery. Anything from silk custom-made underwear to art prints to funky clothing. Open on Saturday from 10am to 5.30pm. Located outdoors in Cow's Lane.
🕂 G7 ✉ Cow's Lane, Temple Bar 🚊 Tara Street 🚌 Cross-city buses

DESIGNYARD
www.designyard.ie
A centre for crafts and decorative arts. The stunning jewellery gallery showcases Irish designers using precious and non-precious materials in many designs.
🕂 G7 ✉ Cow's Lane, Temple Bar ☎ 474 1011 🚊 Tara Street 🚌 Cross-city buses

EAGER BEAVER
Next-to-new clothing with well-known brand names at good prices.
🕂 G7 ✉ Crown Alley, Temple Bar ☎ 677 3342 🚊 Tara Street 🚌 Cross-city buses

FLIP
One of the first ports of call for trendy Irish shoppers on the trail of secondhand jeans, checked shirts, baseball jackets, bowling bags and other bits of Americana.
🕂 G7 ✉ 3–4 Fownes Street Upper, Temple Bar ☎ 671 4299 🚊 Tara Street 🚌 Cross-city buses

GALLIC KITCHEN
Yummy choice of homemade treats from quiches and pies to pastries. Famous over the past 15 years for its salmon and chicken plaits.
🕂 F7 ✉ 49 Francis Street ☎ 454 4912 🚌 Cross-city buses

GEORGE STREET MARKET ARCADE
Covered arcade with everything from secondhand records and books to collectables, olives and a fortune teller.
🕂 G7 ✉ Between South Great George's Street and Drury Street 🚊 Pearse 🚌 Cross-city buses

HARLEQUIN
Classy vintage clothing and accessories, in particular vintage handbags, which are a house specialty.
🕂 G7 ✉ 13 Castle Market ☎ 671 0202 🚊 Pearse 🚌 Cross-city buses

HAUS
One of Dublin's leading contemporary homeware stores, this is where Dublin style gurus pick up designer items and accessories. The premises are entirely ecofriendly with lots of 'green' features.
🕂 G7 ✉ 3–4 Crow Street, off Dame Street ☎ 679 5155 🚊 Tara Street 🚌 Cross-city buses

JENNY VANDER
The place for intricate evening wear, coats, dresses and separates in delicate and luxurious fabrics as well as shoes, handbags and jewellery from another era. It's all more antique than secondhand.
🕂 G7 ✉ 20 George's Street Arcade, South Great George's Street ☎ 677 0406 🚌 Cross-city buses

THE SOUTHWEST

SHOPPING

JOHN FARRINGTON ANTIQUES

This small shop is packed to the gills with Irish furniture, silver, glass and *objets d'art*. The precious antique jewellery is fabulous. Celebrity clientele.

🞧 G7 ✉ 32 Drury Street ☎ 679 1899 🚆 Pearse 🚌 Cross-city buses

NUE BLUE ERIU

www.nueblueriu.com
If you are tired after all your shopping why not try some gorgeous products from this smart shop. Cosmetics and skincare items from around the world. You can also book in for body massage.

🞧 G7 ✉ 7 South William Street ☎ 672 5766 🚆 Pearse 🚌 Cross-city buses

O'SULLIVAN ANTIQUES

www.osullivanantiques.com
A seasoned expert on the Irish antiques scene, Chantal O'Sullivan' has a keen eye for exquisite items from years gone by. Mahogany furniture, gilt mirrors, marble mantelpieces, garden statues and delicate glass.

🞧 F7 ✉ 43–44 Francis Street ☎ 454 1143 🚌 78A, 123

PATAGONIA

www.patagonia.com
This Patagonia shop is the only outlet shop in Europe and is located in a Georgian building. Iconic brand of ecofriendly outdoor wear, with bargains on past seasons gear.

🞧 G7 ✉ 24–26 Exchequer Street ☎ 670 5748 🚌 Cross-city buses

PEEKABOO

For the dress for that special occasion, this shop makes made-to-order beautiful garments in gorgeous materials. Also some ready-to-wear.

🞧 G7 ✉ Unit 7, Crow Street, Temple Bar ☎ 670 3253 🚆 Tara Street 🚌 Cross-city buses

SMOCK

A quirky boutique with designers such as Veronique Branquino, Ali Malek and Easton Pearson, plus Olivia Morris shoes and Scott Wilson jewellery; all at the cutting edge of fashion.

🞧 G7 ✉ Smock Alley Court, East Essex Street ☎ 613 9000

SATURDAY MARKET

Irish food lovers spend Saturday in Meeting House Square at Temple Bar, where the weekly food market sells a variety of produce ranging from Japanese sushi to Mexican burritos. Local Irish produce includes fresh breads, jams, yogurts and vegetables. Those with a sweeter tooth will enjoy the handmade fudge and chocolate stalls or freshly cooked waffles and crêpes. Cheeses, olives, oysters and more.

🚆 Tara Street 🚌 Cross-city buses

TIMEPIECE ANTIQUE CLOCKS

Both selling and restoration goes on at this intriguing shop that is all about 18th- and 19th-century clocks. The emphasis is on Irish longcase clocks but there are some highly decorative French pieces as well.

🞧 F8 ✉ 57–58 St. Patrick's Street ☎ 454 0774 🚌 Cross-city buses

WALTONS

www.waltons.ie
Dublin brims over with music and musicians and Waltons supplies everyone from wannabe rock stars to the stalwarts of the traditional scene. They have been Irish music specialists for more than 75 years. From *bodhráns* to whistles, pipes to accordions, plus sheet music, Irish songbooks and accessories. Another branch is at 2–5 North Frederick Street.

🞧 G7 ✉ 69–70 South Great George's Street ☎ 475 066 🚆 Pearse 🚌 Cross-city buses

WILD CHILD

www.wildchild.ie
Kitschy, quirky vintage clothing, cards, buttons, accessories and cosmetics. Great venue for impersonators' garb.

🞧 G7 ✉ 61 and 77 South Great George's Street ☎ 475 5099 🚌 Cross-city buses

Entertainment and Nightlife

ANDREW'S LANE
www.andrewslanetheatre.com
The main stage and a smaller studio upstairs attract a steady stream of young theatre-goers.
🔷 H7 ✉ 9–17 Andrew's Lane ☎ 679 5720 🚇 Pearse 🚌 Cross-city buses

BRAZEN HEAD
www.brazenhead.com
Reputedly the oldest bar in town (trading for more than 800 years), the Brazen Head has an old-world charm. The walls are covered with memorabilia. Good food, drink and Irish music sessions.
🔷 F7 ✉ 20 Bridge Street Lower ☎ 679 5186 🚌 21

CLUB M
www.club.ie
A lively club in the heart of Temple Bar. Mainly aimed at the up front cruising crowd who boogie into the early hours to mainstream chart hits.
🔷 H7 ✉ Blooms Hotel, 6 Anglesea Street, Temple Bar ☎ 671 5622 🚇 Tara Street 🚌 Cross-city buses

EAMONN DORAN'S
Big Temple Bar venue with dance floors and bars. Mix is house to indie. Some live music.
🔷 G7 ✉ 3a Crown Alley ☎ 679 9114 🚇 Tara Street 🚌 Cross-city buses

FITZSIMONS
www.fitzsimonshotel.com
Dublin's most vibrant and happening nightspot. The Ballroom nightclub has regular theme nights and changing DJs play a mix of pop, dance and chart hits. Traditional Irish music and dance takes place nightly on the ground floor and the upper floor has a riverside restaurant.
🔷 G7 ✉ 21–22 Wellington Quay, Temple Bar ☎ 677 9315 🚇 Tara Street 🚌 Cross-city buses

THE FRONT LOUNGE
Stylish bar with changing artworks on the walls and a mixed crowd: business types by day; arty crowd by evening; and gay and straight twentysomethings late at night.
🔷 G7 ✉ 33–34 Parliament Street ☎ 670 4112 🚇 Tara Street 🚌 Cross-city buses

HOGAN'S
A fashionable bar packed with Dublin's beautiful young things on their way to nearby dance clubs.
🔷 G7 ✉ 35 South Great George's Street ☎ 677 5904 🚌 Cross-city buses

IRISH FILM CENTRE
www.irishfilm.ie
Art films or limited release movies on the two screens in this interesting conversion. Restaurant, bar, shop and movie archive.
🔷 G7 ✉ 6 Eustace Street, Temple Bar ☎ 679 5744 🚇 Tara Street 🚌 Cross-city buses

THE LONG HALL
Time seems to have stood still in this traditional hostelry, with a long bar, smoked glass and lovely paintwork.
🔷 G7 ✉ 51 South Great George's Street ☎ 475 1590 🚌 Cross-city buses

THE NEW THEATRE
Through the Connolly Bookshop, this professional venue for drama showcases new Irish work.
🔷 G7 ✉ 43 Essex Street East, Temple Bar ☎ 670 3361 🚇 Tara Street 🚌 Cross-city buses

OLIVER ST. JOHN GOGARTY
www.gogartys.ie
A pub since the mid-19th century, in the heart of Temple Bar, is a popular venue for traditional music and dance. Good food and great *craic*.
🔷 H6 ✉ 58–59 Fleet Street ☎ 671 1822 🕐 Music daily 🚇 Tara Street 🚌 Cross-city buses

OLYMPIA
Dublin's oldest theatre mounts mainstream

shows including musicals, comedy and pantomimes.
🔢 G7 ✉ 72 Dame Street ☎ 679 3323 🚌 Cross-city buses

O'SHEA'S MERCHANT

www.osheashotel.com
Nightly traditional music and dancing—everyone is encouraged to take to the dance floor. Let your inhibitions go.
🔢 F7 ✉ 12 Lower Bridge Street ☎ 679 3797 🚌 51B, 78A

PALACE BAR

Established in 1843, this traditional pub still retains its old frosted glass and mahogany interior. It was a favourite haunt of many literary giants of Dublin including Brendan Behan, Patrick Kavanagh and W. B. Yeats.
🔢 H6 ✉ 21 Fleet Street ☎ 671 7388 🚌 Cross-city buses

THE PORTERHOUSE

www.porterhousebrewco.com
Opened in 1996, this was Dublin's first microbrewery, and despite new competition is still doing an excellent job. It now brews three ales, three stouts and three lagers and the occasional special, all brewed on the premises. On four separate levels, the food is good here, too, and you may well catch some live music.
🔢 G7 ✉ 16–18 Parliament Street, Temple Bar ☎ 679 8847 🚌 Cross-city buses

PROJECT ARTS CENTRE

www.project.ie
Young theatre groups stage new and experimental performances at lunchtime, in the evening and late at night. A chance for young Irish talent to shine.
🔢 G7 ✉ 39 East Essex Street ☎ 881 963 🚆 Tara Street 🚌 Cross-city buses

RÍ RÁ

www.rira.ie
A good night out. Informal and fashionable with a chill-out area upstairs.
🔢 G7 ✉ Dame Court ☎ 671 1220 🚆 Tara Street 🚌 Cross-city buses

STAG'S HEAD

Built in 1770 and remodelled in 1895, this pub has retained wonderful stained-glass windows,

MOVIE FACTS

● Dublin has one of the highest per capita movie attendances in Europe.
● The Irish Film Centre, the Savoy and the Screen are all venues for the Dublin film festival in March.
● It's cheaper during the day.
● New films are sometimes released earlier in Ireland than in the UK due to the film distribution system.
● On Saturday nights from June to September there are free showings of films at Meeting House Square in Temple Bar.

wood carvings and iron work. Attractively set off a cobblestoned lane.
🔢 G7 ✉ 1 Dame Court ☎ 679 6387 🚌 Cross-city buses

TEMPLE BAR MUSIC CENTRE

www.tbmc.ie
A premier music venue that also stages fashion shows, club nights and dance events. Café, bar and good live music.
🔢 G7 ✉ Curved Street ☎ 670 9202 🚆 Tara Street 🚌 Cross-city buses

VIPER ROOM

Great for jazz, blues and cabaret sessions. There's not a lot of room and seating can be sparse. Downstairs there's an intimate 1970's-style dance floor. Great cocktails and late opening although the doormen can be a bit heavy.
🔢 H6 ✉ 5 Aston Quay ☎ 672 5566 🚌 Cross-city buses

WHELAN'S

www.whelanslive.com
Good acoustics, plenty of space and a great atmosphere. Up-and-coming Irish groups and overseas bands on tour often headline. Licensed to serve alcohol since 1772. Renovation work in the early 1990s revealed the original wood and stonework.
🔢 G8 ✉ 25 Wexford Street ☎ 478 0766 🚆 Pearse 🚌 16, 16A, 19, 19A, 65, 83

Restaurants

AR VICOLETTO OSTERIA ROMANA (€€)

This is one of Dublin's best kept secrets; an authentic taste of Italy in the heart of Temple Bar. Only the freshest of ingredients are used here and you can choose from meat, fish or pasta, accompanied by a good Chianti. You are guaranteed a warm welcome.

✚ G7 ✉ 5 Crow Street, Temple Bar ☎ 670 8662 ◷ Lunch Mon–Sat, dinner daily ▐ Tara Street ▣ Cross-city buses

BAD ASS CAFÉ (€)

www.badasscafe.com
Long-established pizza restaurant that once employed a young Sinead O'Connor as a waitress.

✚ G7 ✉ 9–11 Crown Alley, Temple Bar ☎ 671 2596 ◷ Daily ▐ Tara Street ▣ Cross-city buses

BOTTICELLI (€€)

This is the real thing, an Italian restaurant run by Italians. The interior may be a bit plain but if you book you can get a table overlooking the river. Good honest pizza, pasta, meat and fish dishes from imported Italian ingredients plus some tempting desserts.

✚ G7 ✉ 3 Temple Bar ☎ 672 7289 ◷ Daily ▐ Tara Street ▣ Cross-city buses

THE CEDAR TREE (€€)

Middle Eastern setting where food concentrates on Lebanese dishes and *meze*. Belly-dancing on Saturday nights.

✚ H7 ✉ 11 St. Andrew's Street ☎ 677 2121 ◷ Dinner only ▐ Pearse ▣ Cross-city buses

EDEN (€€)

www.edenrestaurant.ie
Contemporary restaurant with predominantly white decor and huge windows, serving modern Irish food with a Mediterranean slant. Popular on summer evenings and for Sunday lunch when the Temple Bar market is in full swing.

✚ G7 ✉ Meeting House Square ☎ 670 5372 ◷ Lunch and dinner daily ▐ Tara Street ▣ Cross-city buses

ELEPHANT AND CASTLE (€)

www.elephantandcastle.com
Widest breakfast menu in Dublin with straight-forward American cuisine. Expect to wait in a line, especially on Sundays, but it's worth it.

✚ G7 ✉ 18 Temple Bar ☎ 679 3121 ◷ Breakfast, lunch and dinner daily ▐ Tara Street ▣ Cross-city buses

FXB (€€€)

www.fxbrestaurants.com
The Temple Bar branch of this meat eater's heaven; but there's seafood as well. Locally sourced, free range meats.

✚ G7 ✉ 2 Crow Street, Temple Bar ☎ 671 1248 ◷ Dinner daily ▐ Tara Street ▣ Cross-city buses

GALLAGHERS BOXTY HOUSE (€€)

www.boxtyhouse.ie
Traditional food focused around the boxty, an Irish potato pancake with a choice of fillings such as meat, fish or vegetables. Well known for the unusual, but tasty, brownbread ice cream.

✚ G7 ✉ 20–21 Temple Bar ☎ 677 2762 ◷ Lunch and dinner daily ▐ Tara Street ▣ Cross-city buses

IL BACCARO (€€)
Atmospheric trattoria in a 17th-century vaulted cellar. Good Italian fare and great wines straight from the barrel.

🔢 G7 ✉ Diceman's Corner, Meeting House Square ☎ 671 4597 🕐 Lunch Sat, dinner daily 🚇 Tara Street 🚌 Cross-city buses

JUICE (€)
Vegetarian food and juice bar with a globally inspired menu that includes Japanese, Italian, Mexican and Caribbean dishes.

🔢 G7 ✉ 73–83 South Great Georges Street ☎ 475 7856 🕐 Lunch and dinner 🚌 Cross-city buses

LEMON CREPE AND COFFEE CO. (€)
For some of the tastiest and mouthwatering crepes washed down with some great coffees—cappuchinos et al.

🔢 G7 ✉ 66 South William Street ☎ 672 9044 🕐 From 8am 🚇 Pearse 🚌 Cross-city buses

LEO BURDOCK'S (€)
Near Christ Church Cathedral, this Dublin institution sells excellent fish and chips that can be eaten across the road in the cathedral garden.

🔢 G7 ✉ 2 Werburgh Street ☎ 454 0306 🚌 Cross-city buses

LES FRÈRES JACQUES (€€€)
www.lesfreresjacques.com
Excellent French cooking in a stylish but informal setting. The friendly owner and staff are happy to offer advice on the exquisite menu and wines. Centrally located. ▶

🔢 G7 ✉ 74 Dame Street ☎ 679 4555 🕐 Lunch Mon–Fri, dinner daily 🚌 Cross-city buses

LORD EDWARD (€€€)
Dublin's oldest seafood restaurant serving a range of fish dishes, from Galway Bay oysters to Sole Véronique in traditional surroundings.

🔢 F7 ✉ 22 Christchurch Place ☎ 454 2420 🕐 Lunch Mon–Fri, dinner Mon–Sat 🚌 Cross-city buses

MERMAID CAFÉ (€€)
www.mermaid.ie
Traditional Irish fare served in a contemporary minimalist style. Only the purest ingredients used—try the excellent crab cakes.

🔢 G7 ✉ 69–70 Dame Street ☎ 670 8236 🕐 Lunch and dinner daily 🚌 Cross-city buses

MEXICO TO ROME (€)
Unique menu allows you to mix favourite Mexicanos with Italian dishes. Busy.

🔢 G7 ✉ 23 East Essex Street ☎ 677 2727 🕐 Lunch and dinner daily 🚇 Tara Street Cross-city buses

MONGOLIAN BARBEQUE (€€)
www.themongolianbarbeque.com
Offers a unique dining experience—an all-you-can-eat buffet.

🔢 G7 ✉ 7 Anglesea Street ☎ 670 4154 🕐 Daily 🚌 Cross-city buses

MONTY'S OF KATHMANDU (€€)
www.montys.ie
The city's only Nepalese restaurant, located in Temple Bar, offers intruiging dishes using secret ingredients. It draws people from a wide area and is enhanced by the friendly staff who give advice on food choices.

🔢 G7 ✉ 28 Eustace Street ☎ 670 4911 🕐 Lunch Mon–Sat, dinner daily 🚇 Tara Street 🚌 Cross-city buses

ODESSA LOUNGE & GRILL (€)
This 1970s-inspired restaurant attracts a hip clientele. A favourite for late Sunday brunch.

EXOTIC TASTES

In Dublin today there has been a notable surge in the number of European, Eastern and Far Eastern restaurants. French, Italian and Mediterranean fare, Scandinavian specialties, Russian, Indian, Japanese and Oriental dishes—the choice from around the world is endless. Other restaurants with an international taste include Lebanese, Filipino, Mexican and for something entirely different there is even a Mongolian barbeque.

✚ G7 ✉ 13–14 Dame Court ☎ 670 7634 ⏰ Brunch and dinner Sat, Sun, dinner Mon–Fri 🚉 Pearse 🚌 Cross-city buses

QUEEN OF TARTS (€)

Traditional tea shop offering a mouthwatering array of homemade cakes, biscuits and tasty baking. Not to be missed.
✚ G7 ✉ Cork Hill, Dame Street ☎ 670 7499 ⏰ Daily 🚉 Tara Street 🚌 Cross-city buses

THE SHACK (€€)

www.shackrestaurant.ie
A cosy Temple Bar restaurant offering wholesome dishes using the best fresh ingredients.
✚ G7 ✉ 24 East Essex Street ☎ 679 0043 ⏰ Lunch and dinner daily 🚉 Tara Street 🚌 Cross-city buses

SHALIMAR (€€)

Innovative cooking from the different regions of India is served in the formal candlelit restaurant. Balti option downstairs.
✚ G7 ✉ 17 South Great Georges Street ☎ 671 0738 ⏰ Lunch Mon–Fri, dinner daily 🚉 Pearse 🚌 Cross-city buses

TANTE ZOE'S (€€)

www.tantezoes.com
For Cajun/Creole cooking; you won't find better gumbos and jambalayas this side of the Mississippi.
✚ G7 ✉ 1a Crow Street, Temple Bar ☎ 679 4407 ⏰ Daily 🚌 Cross-city buses

THE TEA ROOM AT THE CLARENCE (€€€)

www.theclarence.ie
High ceilings and crisp white table cloths set the scene in this upscale, up-to-the-minute celebs hotel owned by the rock group U2.
✚ G7 ✉ The Clarence, 6–8 Wellington Quay ☎ 670 8343 ⏰ Lunch Sun–Fri, dinner daily 🚌 Cross-city buses

THAI ORCHID (€€)

Spread over three floors you will get all the established Thai specials here; well cooked and presented. Authentic decor and meals are served by courteous Thai staff in traditional costume.
✚ H6 ✉ 7 Westmoreland Street ☎ 671 9969 ⏰ Lunch Mon–Fri, dinner daily 🚌 Cross-city buses

---

IN VOGUE

Dublin's reputation as a fashionable youth-orientated city is borne out by the capital's cosmopolitan restaurant scene. Listed on these pages are the city's most popular haunts and you should try and make reservations as far ahead as possible. Many of Dublin's trendier restaurants have two evening seatings on weekends. The early seating is usually around 7pm while the later seating is from 9.30ish. If you want to linger, check your table's not booked for a second party.

THOMAS READ (€)

Brasserie with an extensive menu of imaginative, freshly prepared home-style dishes. One of the best pub lunches in town.
✚ G7 ✉ 1–4 Parliament Street ☎ 671 7283 ⏰ Food served at lunch only 🚌 Cross-city buses

TRASTEVERE (€€)

www.trastevere.ie
Upbeat eatery that blends Italian food with a taste of New York.
✚ G7 ✉ Unit 1 Temple Bar Square ☎ 407 0813 ⏰ Lunch and dinner daily 🚉 Tara Street 🚌 Cross-city buses

UKIYO BAR (€€€)

www.ukiyobar.com
Dublin's first and only sake bar and karaoke box venue that serves good modern Asian cuisine in the restaurant upstairs. Be prepared to eat on low tables and expect to be encouraged to share dishes and experiment with tastes.
✚ G7 ✉ 7–9 Exchequer Street ☎ 633 4071 ⏰ Lunch Mon–Sat, dinner daily 🚉 Tara Street 🚌 Cross-city buses

YAMAMORI (€)

Japanese noodle and sushi house frequented by young Dubliners. Good choice of dishes to suit all palates.
✚ G7 ✉ 71–72 South Great Georges Street ☎ 475 5001 ⏰ Lunch and dinner daily 🚌 Cross-city buses

Although run down by the 1990s the area north of the River Liffey has been undergoing a face life and the famous O'Connell Street has been smartened up. Smithfield is developing as the latest fashionable district.

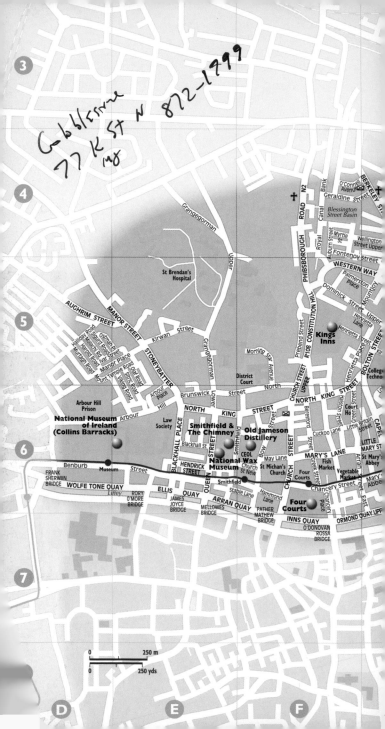

Collins Barracks

The striking building of Collins Barracks contains a fine collection of decorative arts

THE BASICS

www.museum.ie
+ E6
✉ Benburb Street
☎ 677 7444
🕐 Tue–Sat 10–5, Sun 2–5
🍴 Café
🚇 Heuston; Luas Heuston
🚌 25, 25A, 40, 66, 67
♿ Very good
✋ Free
❓ Book tours in advance (inexpensive)

HIGHLIGHTS

● Old barracks building
● Fonthill vase
● Multi-storey clock
● 'The Way We Wore' exhibition
● Curator's Choice

Here you can view the decorative arts and social history collections of the National Museum—products of Irish artists and craftspeople that have been hidden from view for many years.

The Building Sir Thomas Burgh (1670–1730), best known as architect of the Old Library in Trinity College (▷ 72–73), also designed Dublin's large Royal Barracks, just over a mile outside the city. Built in 1704, on high ground overlooking the River Liffey, they were handed over in 1922 to the Irish State, which named them after Michael Collins, the revolutionary leader killed in an ambush towards the end of the Civil War. Until decommissioning in 1997, they were generally thought to be the oldest military barracks still in use anywhere in the world.

Exhibits The barracks opened as an annex to the National Museum in the same year, greatly strengthening Dublin's cultural and historical focus. The items on display range from the 17th century to the present day and comprise Irish silver, glass and furniture, all of which reached a high point of artistic excellence, particularly in the 18th century. Don't miss the Chinese porcelain Fonthill vase, which has managed to survive its well-documented wanderings in Asia and Europe, or the clock whose winding chains extend the height of two floors. Opened in 2000, the permanent exhibition of 250 years of Irish clothing and jewellery, 'The Way We Wore', expands on how the Irish echoed the styles of the fashion conscious of Europe.

Dublin City Gallery The Hugh Lane

Studying at the Hugh Lane (left). The Punt by Jean-Baptiste-Camille Corot (right)

Degas, Monet, Corot and Renoir are among the Impressionist artists whose paintings are on display in this gallery that also looks back over 100 years of Irish art, including paintings and stained glass.

Philanthropist The Hugh Lane Gallery fills a niche between the old masters on display in the National Gallery (▷ 65) and the ultramodern creations in the Irish Museum of Modern Art (▷ 96) at Kilmainham. Built between 1761 and 1763 by the Earl of Charlemont to the designs of Sir William Chambers, the gallery now bears the name of Sir Hugh Lane who was drowned when the Lusitania sank in 1915. Before his death, Sir Hugh added a codicil to his will stating that a group of 39 of his Impressionist pictures that were in London, including works by Corot, Degas, Manet, Monet and Renoir, should go to Dublin. However, the codicil was unwitnessed with the result that London claimed the canvases and kept them until it was agreed that each city should display half of them at any time in rotation. The gallery has doubled in size since its reopening in May 2006. You can also visit the reconstructed studio of Francis Bacon, complete with its entire contents of more than 7,500 items.

Modern art Irish artists of the last hundred years, including Osborne, Yeats, Orpen, Henry and Le Brocquy, are well represented, and modern European artists include Beuys and Albers. Make sure you see the stunning examples of stained glass by Clarke, Home and Scanlon.

THE BASICS

www.hughlane.ie
🕂 G5
✉ Charlemont House Parnell Square North
☎ 874 1903
🕐 Tue–Thu 9.30–6, Fri, Sat 9.30–5, Sun 11–5
🍴 Café
🚆 Connolly
🚌 Cross-city buses
♿ Good
✋ Free; Bacon Studio expensive

HIGHLIGHTS

● Impressionist paintings
● Jack Yeats, *There is no Night*
● Orpen, *Homage to Manet*
● Works by Roderic O'Connor
● Stained glass
● Francis Bacon's studio

Dublin Writers Museum

The Writer's Gallery (left). Modern stained-glass window (middle). Children's room (right)

THE BASICS

www.writersmuseum.com
➕ G5
✉ 18 Parnell Square North
☎ 872 2077
🕐 Jun–end Aug Mon–Fri 10–6, Sat 10–5, Sun 11–5; Sep–end May Mon–Sat 10–5, Sun 11–5
🍴 Café; Chapter One restaurant downstairs
🚉 Connolly Station
🚌 Cross-city buses
♿ Ground floor good (a few steps into the building)
💷 Expensive
❓ Audio guide. Combined tickets available

HIGHLIGHTS

● Letters of Thomas Moore and Maria Edgeworth
● Yeats manuscript
● Indenture signed by Swift

For centuries a meeting point for gifted writers, Dublin has become the hub of a great literary tradition. This museum celebrates their diverse talents and displays a truly fascinating range of memorabilia.

Great Irish writers Many languages have been spoken by Ireland's inhabitants down the centuries, including Norse, Irish and Norman French, but it was with the establishment of English as the *lingua franca* in the 17th century that Dublin's literary reputation was established. Restoration dramatists such as George Farquhar were followed 50 years later by the brilliance and acerbic wit of Jonathan Swift. At the end of the 19th century, a new era dawned with the emergence of Oscar Wilde, whose epigrams enthralled the world. Around the turn of the 20th century, William Butler Yeats, encouraged by the flourishing Irish literary movement, helped found the Abbey Theatre, which opened in 1904. His contemporary, George Bernard Shaw, and subsequent Irish writers such as James Joyce, Samuel Beckett and Brendan Behan have continued to open new horizons in world literature.

Displays Photographs, paintings and other items linked with Ireland's literary titans are backed up with lots of explanatory material. First editions and rare volumes abound, and there are original letters of the poet Thomas Moore, a manuscript of W. B. Yeats and an indenture signed by Jonathan Swift. Take time to have a look at the house itself.

James Joyce Centre

Of all the literati to grace the Dublin scene during the 20th century, James Joyce has undoubtedly earned the greatest reputation internationally, so it is fitting that a whole house is devoted to the writer and his work.

Connections This 18th-century house, in an impressive street of equally well-restored Georgian redbrick residences just 275m (300 yards) from O'Connell Street, is home to the James Joyce Centre. Initially, its Joycean connection was established through a dancing master called Denis J. Maginni, who leased one of the rooms in the house around the turn of the 20th century and appears as a character in Ulysses. A more immediate connection is the presence of members of the novelist's family, including his nephew Ken Monaghan, who shows visitors around the house and gives them the opportunity to listen to tapes of Uncle James, reading from Ulysses and Finnegan's Wake.

Memorabilia Take time out to browse in the extensive library and gaze at the portraits of those featured in the master's work, either under their own name or a pseudonym. You can also see the original doorway rescued from the now-demolished No. 7 Eccles Street, the imagined residence of the Ulyssean hero Leopold Bloom, in the courtyard, which also displays murals based on Ulysses. The centre is also a starting point for an hour-long walking tour (payable separately) of Joycean sites on the north side of the city.

THE BASICS

www.jamesjoyce.ie
H5
35 North Great Georges Street
878 8547
Mon–Fri 9.30–12.30, 1.30–3.30
Connolly
Cross-city buses
Few
Moderate
Guided tours of house and Joycean Dublin

HIGHLIGHTS

- Joyce family members
- Recordings
- Library
- Portraits of characters in Ulysses
- No. 7 Eccles Street door

THE NORTH

★

TOP 25

51

O'Connell Street

HIGHLIGHTS

● Portico decoration, statues and plaques of the General Post Office
● The Spire
● Clery's department store
● Easons bookshop
● Daniel O'Connell statue

An impressive, tree lined thoroughfare, O'Connell Street leads down to the River Liffey and the always busy O'Connell Bridge. Full of monuments and historic public buildings, it has witnessed some memorable events in Irish history.

Grandiose monuments Two monuments dominate either end of O'Connell Street. Close to the bridge over the Liffey, is the mighty statue of Daniel O'Connell, passionate supporter of Catholic emancipation for Ireland. At the northern end is the monument to Charles Stewart Parnell, the leader of the struggle for Irish Home Rule.

General Post Office This building symbolizes the birthplace of modern Ireland. Its classical splendour was designed by Francis Johnston

The General Post Office (left) in O'Connell Street—scene of a major incident during the Easter Rising of 1916
Detail from the statue and monument to Daniel O'Connell (right) on the street that bears his name

(1814–18), with statues by John Smith that dominate the skyline. Inside the reading of the Proclamation of the Irish Republic took place during the Easter Rising of 1916. The insurgents were forced to surrender after the interior was reduced to rubble (the bullet chips on the portico columns are a sobering reminder of the bitter struggle) and 16 were later executed. However, their stand led to the creation of modern Ireland and a salute is given here in their memory at Dublin's annual St. Patrick's Day parade.

Monument of Light More commmonly known as the Spire, this striking modern edifice was unveilled in September 2002. Erected on the site across the road from the General Post Office where Nelson's Column used to be, it is made of stainless steel and is 120m (393ft) high.

THE BASICS

General Post Office
✚ H5
✉ O'Connell Street
☎ 872 8888
🕐 Mon–Sat 8–8, Sun and public hols 10.30–6
🚉 Tara Street
🚌 Cross-city buses
♿ Few
🎫 Free

More to See

CUSTOM HOUSE
Designed by James Gandon in 1791, the Custom House is an outstanding example of Georgian architecture and one of Dublin's finest buildings. The visitor centre has a museum with displays on Gandon's work and the building's history. Look out for more examples of Gandon's work around the city.

➕ J6 ✉ Custom House Quay ☎ 888 2538 🕐 Mid-Mar to end Nov Mon–Fri 10–12.30, Sat, Sun 2–5; Nov to mid-Mar Wed–Fri 10–12.30, Sun 2–5 🚉 Tara Street 🚌 Cross-city buses ♿ Good 💷 Inexpensive

FAMINE FIGURES
A series of emaciated figures along the quays commemorates the Great Famine of 1845–49. Plaques bearing the names of families who suffered will be added over time. (The sculptor, Rowan Gillespie, is also behind the 'Spiderman' scaling the Treasury Building on Grand Canal Street.)

➕ J6 ✉ Custom House Quay 🚉 Tara Street 🚌 Cross-city buses

FOUR COURTS
Home to the Irish law courts since 1796, the Four Courts has much in common with the Custom House— primarily its designer, James Gandon. The building also suffered fire damage (as did the Custom House) during the turbulent events of 1921. Visits are only when courts are in session.

➕ F6 ✉ Inns Quay ☎ 872 5555 🚌 Cross-city buses ♿ Few 💷 Free

GARDEN OF REMEMBRANCE
The statue of the Children of Lír is the focal point of this contemplative garden, dedicated to those who died in pursuit of Irish independence. A poignant Irish fairy tale, about three children turned into swans by a wicked stepmother, inspired Oisín Kelly's bronze sculpture (1971).

➕ G5 ✉ Garden of Remembrance, Parnell Square East ☎ 874 3074 🚌 Cross-city buses

GRESHAM HOTEL
www.gresham-hotels.com
Once Dublin's grandest hotel, steeped

The Children of Lír

The copper dome of the Custom House

in history. In the 1960s, the Beatles played an impromptu session here, the band's only live performance in Ireland. The forming of the Chieftains, Ireland's greatest exponents of traditional music, also happened here in the 1960s.

➕ H5 ✉ 23 O'Connell Street Upper ☎ 874 6881 🚌 Cross-city buses

KING'S INNS

The honorable society of the King's Inns is the impressive setting for Dublin law students training for the bar. Steeped in tradition, this beautiful building was begun by James Gandon. Tours by prior arrangement.

➕ F5 ✉ Henrietta Street ☎ 874 4840 🚌 25, 25A, 66, 67, 83, 90 ♿ Few 🖐 Free

NATIONAL WAX MUSEUM

The museum brings to life everyone from Irish historical figures to the cult cartoon family the Simpsons. Attractions include the Hall of the Megastars and Chamber of Horrors.

➕ E6 ✉ Smithfield Square ☎ 872 6340 🕐 Closed at time of writing–due to open early 2007; call for times and prices 🚌 83 🚊 Luas Smithfield

OLD JAMESON DISTILLERY

www.whiskeytours.ie

Explore the history of Irish whiskey-making through exhibits and audio-visual presentations on the site of the old Jameson Distillery. Sample a drop of the *uisce beatha*, literally 'water of life', at the visitor bar—included in the ticket. Guided tours only.

➕ F6 ✉ Bow Street, Smithfield ☎ 807 2355 🕐 Daily 9.30–6. Tours every 40 mins; last tour 5.30 🍴 Visitor bar 🚌 68, 69, 79, 83, 90; Luas Smithfield ♿ Good 🖐 Expensive

SMITHFIELD

Once notoriously run down, this corner of Dublin is reinventing itself since its initial redevelopment in the 1990s and now has shops, restaurants and new apartments. Highlights include the Old Jameson Distillery (▷ above) and the 56m (185 ft) high Chimney (▷ 4).

➕ F6 ✉ Smithfield 🚌 83 🚊 Luas Smithfield

The Mansion House on Dawson Street

The view from the Chimney, Smithfield

A Walk North of the River

This walk is in the lesser known northern district of Dublin, undergoing a major rejuvenation. It also takes in part of the quays.

DISTANCE: 2km (1.25 miles) **ALLOW:** 1 hour plus stops

START

GPO, O'CONNELL STREET (▷ 52)
🚏 H6 🚌 Cross-city buses

1 Start at the General Post Office (▷ 52) in O'Connell Street and then look up for the Spire monument (▷ 53), which towers above the street and sways gently in the breeze.

2 Opposite the Spire go left into Henry Street. Halfway down you will find the two shopping malls, the Ilac and the Jervis (▷ 57). This area has been considerably smartened up.

3 Continue along into Mary Street and at the T-junction at the end turn left into Capel Street. Walk on over two roads down to the quayside.

4 In front of you is the Grattan Bridge with its fine sculpted seahorses. Turn right along the quay, passing the next bridge, O'Donovan Rossa Bridge, and into Inns Quay.

END

SMITHFIELD VILLAGE (▷ 55)
🚏 E6 🚌 83 and Luas Smithfield

8 Take the passageway through to Smithfield Square to ascend the old distillery Chimney (▷ 4, 55) for a great view of the city.

7 At the end turn right into Bow Street where you will find the Old Jameson Distillery (▷ 55). You can pause here to take a tour, sample a glass of whiskey or have coffee or lunch. Here, too, is Duck Lane with an interiors shop and restaurants.

6 Take the next right, Church Street. Cross the road and you will see St. Michan's church on your left, famous for the mummified bodies in its crypt. Continue to the traffic lights and turn left into May Lane.

5 To your right is the fine Georgian building of the Four Courts (▷ 54).

Shopping

ARNOTTS

This large department store stocks everything from the traditional to the fashionable in clothes, interiors, household, leisure, entertainment and cosmetics.

➕ G6 ✉ Henry Street ☎ 805 0400 🚉 Connolly 🚌 Cross-city buses; Luas Jervis

CHINA SHOWROOMS

www.chinashowrooms.ie
Old-fashioned shop with displays of well-known names in china and crystal glassware and bargains galore.

➕ H6 ✉ 32 Abbey Street Lower ☎ 878 6211 🚉 Tara Street 🚌 Cross-city buses

CLERY'S

www.clerys.ie
A Dublin institution. Many romantic assignations have been made beneath the clock outside this store. Refurbishment has brightened it up.

➕ H6 ✉ O'Connell Street, ☎ 878 6000 🚉 Tara Street 🚌 Cross-city buses

DUBLIN WOOLLEN MILLS

www.woollenmills.com
Great selection of sweaters, kilts, shawls, accessories and crafts.

➕ G6 ✉ 41 Ormond Quay Lower ☎ 677 5014 🚉 Tara Street 🚌 Cross-city buses

DUBLIN WRITERS MUSEUM BOOKSHOP

www.writersmuseum.com
This excellent shop, in the home of literary Dublin, covers all aspects of Irish writing from travel to poetry, including works by many of the writers featured in the museum.

➕ G5 ✉ 18 Parnell Street North ☎ 872 2077 🚉 Connolly 🚌 Cross-city buses

EASON'S

www.easons.ie
This vast bookstore has a huge selection of books and magazines together with stationery, art equipment and music. Café. Several branches, including one near Trinity College.

➕ H6 ✉ 40 O'Connell Street ☎ 858 3800 🚉 Tara Street or Connolly 🚌 Cross-city buses

THE EPICUREAN FOOD HALL

Homemade ice cream, sweet pastries, bagels, vegetarian and organic sellers contend with each other for the most divine

smells each day.

➕ G6 ✉ Liffey Street Upper 🚉 Tara Street 🚌 Cross-city buses

ILAC CENTRE

Dublin's longest established shopping mall has had a face-lift. The labyrinth of smaller shops and a branch of Dunnes department store surround the County Library.

➕ G6 ✉ Henry Street ☎ 704 1460 🚉 Tara Street 🚌 Cross-city buses; Luas Jervis

JERVIS CENTRE

www.jervis.ie
You will find most British chain stores, including a huge Debenhams and Marks & Spencer at this modern shopping malll covering several floors. The upper floor is a vast food court. Popular with Dubliners, especially with the introduction of the Luas tram system.

➕ G6 ✉ Jervis Street ☎ 878 1323 🚉 Tara Street 🚌 Cross-city buses; Luas Jervis

ROCHES

www.roches-stores.ie
Roches department store started life in 1900 in Cork and opened on this site in Henry Street in 1927. Now one of Ireland's leading stores, it sells a range of fashion, homeware, gifts and food.

➕ G6 ✉ Henry Street ☎ 873 0044 🚉 Tara Street 🚌 Cross-city buses; Luas Jervis

Entertainment and Nightlife

ABBEY
www.abbeytheatre.ie
The national theatre played a vital role in the renaissance of Irish culture at the end of the 19th century. The quality of playwriting and performances is rarely surpassed. Many first runs go to New York's Broadway or London's West End.
➕ H6 ✉ 26 Abbey Street Lower ☎ 878 7222
🚉 Connolly/Tara Street
🚌 Cross-city buses

AMBASSADOR
Small live music venue. Visiting acts include international big names.
➕ H5 ✉ Parnell Street
☎ 878 6796 🚌 Cross-city buses

CINEWORLD
www.cineworld.ie
Formally known as the Parnell Centre, this multiplex has 17 screens. Entertainment includes simulated rides, computer games, themed bars and restaurants, fast-food outlets, virtual reality experiences and a parking area. You could spend hours here without catching a glimpse of daylight.
➕ G6 ✉ Parnell Centre, Parnell Street ☎ 872 8444/872 8400 🚉 Connolly
🚌 Cross-city buses

GATE
www.gatetheatre.ie
Some of Dublin's most inspired and sophisticated theatre, performed in an 18th-century building.

Many Dublin thespians and critics rate the works performed here as the best in Ireland.
➕ G5 ✉ Parnell Square
☎ 874 4045 🚉 Connolly
🚌 Cross-city buses

THE ICE BAR
There's a lot going on here with live music on Friday and Saturday night, a DJ playing and a big screen for sport. There's also a beer garden with Asian and Chinese beer.
➕ H5 ✉ 104 Parnell Street
☎ 8873 4330 🚌 Cross-city buses

MORRISON'S BAR
www.morrisonhotel.ie
Stylish, top celeb-spotting venue where all the beautiful, sexy people hang out.
➕ G6 ✉ Ormond Quay Lower ☎ 887 2400
🚌 Cross-city buses

DANCE
When looking for the best dance clubs in Dublin, go by the name of that particular night at the club rather than the name of the venue itself. Most good dance nights are independently run gigs organized by promoters and staged in different places around town. *The Event Guide,* distributed free in bars and cafés around the city, has the most comprehensive and accurate listings. The Tourist Information Office will also help you find your best venue.

MURPHY'S LAUGHTER LOUNGE
Treat yourself to a good giggle with a host of local international stand-up talent staged on Thursday, Friday and Saturday.
➕ H6 ✉ 4–6 Eden Quay
☎ 874 4611 🚉 Tara Street
🚌 Cross-city buses

PEACOCK
www.abbeytheatre.ie
The Abbey's younger sibling located in the same complex is a platform for emerging Irish talent.
➕ H6 ✉ 26 Abbey Street Lower ☎ 878 7222
🚉 Connolly/Tara Street
🚌 Cross-city buses

THE POINT
www.thepoint.ie
Vast venue in a former tram depot and a premier arena for the top music and dance superstars.
➕ M6 ✉ East Link Bridge, North Wall Quay ☎ 836 6777 🚌 53A

REDZ BAR
www.redzbar.ie
Red is the theme of the ground floor cocktail lounge. Live DJ nightly.
➕ H6 ✉ O'Connell Street Bridge 🚉 Connolly/Tara Street 🚌 Cross-city buses

SAVOY
www.savoy.ie
This old-style movie theatre hosts most Irish movie premieres and their parties. Modern concessions include five wide screens, drink holders and Dolby sound systems.

🚇 H5 ✉ O'Connell Street
☎ 874 6000 🚋 Connolly
🚌 Cross-city buses

SPIRIT

Dance club that brings a whole new approach. On three floors you can dance to your favourite sound—house, soul, reggae, funk, etc. or chill out downstairs with cool sounds and holistic treatments.
🚇 H6 ✉ 57 Abbey Street Middle ☎ 877 9999 🚋 Tara Street 🚌 Cross-city buses

THE VAULTS

www.thevaults.ie
A mainstream nightclub in the International Financial Services Centre, with Smooth Grooves, hip-hop, R & B on Friday nights; R & B and 1980s soul on Saturday nights.
🚇 J5 ✉ IFSC, under Connolly Station ☎ 605 4700
🚋 Connolly 🚌 Cross-city buses

Restaurants

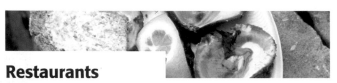

PRICES

Prices are approximate, based on a 3-course meal for one person.
€€€   over €40
€€   €20–€40
€   under €20

COBALT CAFÉ (€)

Good for light snacks and art lovers. Airy café with artworks on the walls. The generously filled sandwiches and tasty cakes keep you going.
🚇 H5 ✉ 16 North Great George's Street ☎ 873 0313
🕐 Mon–Fri 10–4pm
🚋 Connolly 🚌 Cross-city buses

HALO (€€€)

www.morrisonhotel.ie
Try this for a memorable dining experience. Succulent Irish/Asian fusion cooking in a sensational atrium setting. Said to be some of the best food in Dublin.
🚇 G6 ✉ Morrison Hotel, Ormond Quay Lower ☎ 887 2400 🕐 Daily lunch and dinner; Sat, Sun breakfast
🚌 Cross-city buses

JOHN M. KEATING (€–€€€)

www.jmk.ie
In a former church, John Keating opened its doors to a new congregation in December 2005. This bar, café and restaurant is great value serving good food in spectacular surroundings

A GOOD CATCH

Fresh fish is plentiful in Dublin restaurants. Oysters, mussels, crab, prawns (shrimps), salmon, ray, mackerel, sole, whiting and trout are all found in local waters. For a truly Irish gastronomic experience, wash down a dozen fresh oysters with a glass of Guinness and mop up the salty juices with home-baked brown bread.

complete with massive church organ.
🚇 G6 ✉ Mary Street
☎ 828 0102 🕐 Lunch, dinner daily 🚋 Luas Smithfield
🚌 83

KELLY & PING (€€)

www.kellyandping.ie
East meets west at this restaurant in a contemporary setting in the heart of Smithfield Village. Asian and European cuisine using fresh local produce. Light lunch option.
🚇 F6 ✉ Smithfield Village
☎ 817 3840 🕐 Lunch Mon–Fri 12–4, dinner Mon–Sat 4pm–late 🚋 Luas Smithfield
🚌 83

OLD JAMESON DISTILLERY (€€)

Wholesome Irish dishes in the restaurant; lighter snacks in the bar—soups and sandwiches.
🚇 F6 ✉ Smithfield Village
☎ 807 2355 🕐 Lunch Mon–Fri, dinner daily 🚋 Luas Smithfield 🚌 83

This district, south of the River Liffey, has been Dublin's most elegant and fashionable area since the 18th century. Here you will find Trinity College, the national museums and stunning Georgian squares.

5

6

Liffey

BUTT
BRIDGE

TALBOT
MEMORIAL
BRIDGE

O'CONNELL
BRIDGE

BURGH QUAY

GEORGE'S QUAY

D'OLIER STREET

Hawkins St

Poolbeg
Street

Cinema

TARA STREET

D

TARA
STREET
STATION

Luke St

Moss St

Gloucester
South

STREET

TOWNSEND

Mark St

Mark's Lar.

COLLEGE
STREET

PEARSE

STREET

7

Trinity College &
The Book of Kells

GRAFTON ST

Douglas Hyde
Gallery

Molly
Malone
Statue

NASSAU STREET

LEINSTER STREET SOUTH

College
Park

Dental
Hospital

LINCOLN PLACE

WESTLAND ROW

Oscar Wilde
House

Clarendon Street

Duke St

street

DAWSON STREET

Frederick St S

Setana Pl

P

CLARE STREET

Heraldic
Museum

National
Library

WEST

Oscar
Wilde
Statue

School
of Music

Chatham
Street

Grafton

Anne St S

MOLESWORTH
ST

St Ann's

KILDARE ST

Leinster
House

National
Gallery of
Ireland

SOUTH

Gaiety
Theatre

King St South

Royal Irish
Academy
Library

Schoolhouse
Lane

Mansion
House

P

National
Museum
of Ireland

Mercer St Lwr

P

Stephen's
Green Centre

Glovers

St Stephen's
Green

Natural History
Museum

MERRION STREET UPPER

Fitzwilliam Lan.

York Street

Alley

Fusilier's
Arch

NORTH

Viking
Splash
Tours

Shelbourne
Hotel

MERRION ROW

The Royal
College of
Surgeons

Mercer St Upr

Cuffe lane

WEST

St Stephen's
Green

EAST

Hume
Street

Ely Place

Ely
House

PEMBROKE STREET UPPER

CUFFE STREET

SOUTH

RHA
Gallagher
Gallery

Pembroke
Lane

Montague
Street

University
Church

Stokes
Place

Newman
House

Iveagh
House

EAST

Leeson Lane

Quin's Lane

LEESON STREET UPPER

Mackie's
Place

PEMBROKE ST WEST

Fitzwilliam
Square
South

FITZWILLIAM PLACE EAST

FITZW

Camden
Place

Iveagh
Gardens

National
Concert Hall

University College

EARLSFORT TERRACE

LEESON STREET LOWER

North

Kingram
place

Cumberland
Road

Lad lane Upr

HARCOURT STREET

HATCH STREET UPPER

Harcourt

Hatch Street Lower

Hatch La

Hatch Place

Leeson
Place

Wilton

N11

MESPIL

8

9

ADELAIDE
ROAD

Eye & Ear
Hospital

G

H

J

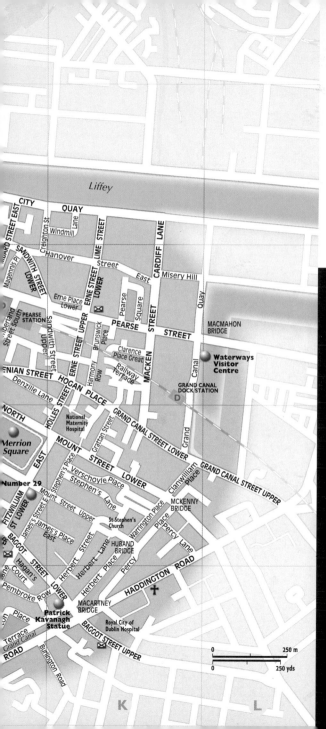

Liffey

CITY QUAY

Windmill Lane

Creighton St

SANDWITH STREET LOWER

Magennis Pl

Hanover Street East

LIME STREET

ERNE STREET LOWER

CARDIFF LANE

Misery Hill

PEARSE STATION

Sandwith Street Upper

Sunderland Street South

Erne Place Lower

ERNE STREET UPPER

Pearse Square

Brunswick Place

PEARSE STREET

MACKEN STREET

Canal Quay

MACMAHON BRIDGE

Clarence Place Great

Railway Terrace

Harmony Row

Waterways Visitor Centre

ENIAN STREET

HOGAN PLACE

Denzille Lane

GRAND CANAL DOCK STATION

D

HOLLES STREET

NORTH

Merrion Square

MERRION SQUARE EAST

National Maternity Hospital

Grattan Street

GRAND CANAL STREET LOWER

Grand Canal

Clanwilliam Place

GRAND CANAL STREET UPPER

Number 29

MOUNT STREET LOWER

Stephen's Place

Verschoyle Place

Stephen's Lane

Mount Street Upper

Warrington Place

MCKENNY BRIDGE

Percy Place

FITZWILLIAM ST LOWER

James's Street East

James's Place East

St Stephen's Church

Percy Lane

BAGGOT STREET

Hagan's Court

Herbert Street

Herbert Lane

HUBAND BRIDGE

Herbert Place

Percy Place

HADDINGTON ROAD

Pembroke Row

Place

MACARTNEY BRIDGE

Patrick Kavanagh Statue

Royal City of Dublin Hospital

Terrace

Grand Canal

ROAD

Burlington Road

BAGGOT STREET UPPER

0 — 250 m

0 — 250 yds

K

L

Heraldic Museum

Medieval banners (left) and monkeys at play on the columns (right) of the Heraldic Museum

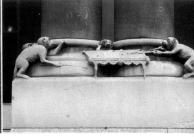

THE BASICS

www.nli.ie

🔢 J7

✉ 2–3 Kildare Street

☎ 603 0311

🕐 Mon–Wed 10–8.30, Thu, Fri 10–4.30, Sat 10–12.30

🚉 Pearse

🚌 Cross-city buses

♿ None

💲 Free

HIGHLIGHTS

● Animal sculptures on façade

● Irish Chieftains Banners

● Flags of Irish infantry in France

● Arms of Napoleon

● Heraldic Insignia Exhibition

Every year, thousands of people come to Ireland in search of their roots, but even those without a drop of Irish blood will find this museum fascinating.

Heraldry The Heraldic Museum, an integral part of the National Library, is housed in Dublin's most colourful mid-19th-century building—the former Kildare Street Club (1858–61), designed by Benjamin Woodward. (The decorative birds and amusing monkeys playing billiards and musical instruments among the window carvings are enough to make a visit worthwhile.) The museum occupies the club's former dining room, beneath the tall ceiling off which hang modern banners of Ireland's ancient chieftain families. Heraldry is on the livery buttons of gentlemen's servants, on the crest of the Joyce clan of Galway, or on items of 19th-century Belleek pottery decorated with the coats of arms of Irish towns. Look for the flags of the Irish infantry regiments who fought in France during the 18th century as well as the mantle and insignia of the knightly Order of St. Patrick.

Napoleon Despite the emphasis on Irish family history, there are also objects from outside Ireland. You will find the arms of the city of Cologne, along with those of the Spencer-Churchill family (late 18th-century), Napoleon Bonaparte and Sir Francis Drake. The 14th-century crusader badge made of pewter is another intriguing item. If you are inspired to trace your own Irish ancestry, ask at the Consultancy Service of the National Library, a few doors along.

Views of the striking National Gallery fronted by its founder, William Dargan

Ireland's National Gallery enjoys considerable standing on the international scene as the home of one of Europe's premier collections of old masters.

Origins Facing onto Merrion Square the National Gallery is set in relaxing green surroundings. The gallery was established in 1854 and opened in 1864 to display old master paintings as an inspiration to budding Irish artists of the mid-Victorian period. Its contents have expanded 20-fold in the century-and-a-half since then, helped by numerous bequests. These include works by Vermeer, Velázquez and Murillo; the legacy of one-third of George Bernard Shaw's residual estate enabled the Gallery to acquire important works by Fragonard and J. L. David, among others.

Masterpieces The Irish paintings, on the ground floor, show a progression from the 18th century onwards while the old masters, for which the gallery is famous, are on the next floor. Wide coverage is given to most European schools of painting—including icons, early Italians (Uccello and Fra Angelico), Renaissance (Titian, Tintoretto), Dutch and Flemish (Rembrandt, Rubens), Spanish (Goya), French (Poussin) and British (Reynolds and Raeburn, among others). The display also covers Impressionists and modern painters up to Picasso. One room is devoted to watercolours and drawings—including 31 by Turner shown every January. The Millennium Wing, opened in 2002, houses an area for the study of Irish art, temporary exhibition galleries and works of Jack B. Yeats.

THE BASICS

www.nationalgallery.ie
➕ J7
✉ Merrion Square West
☎ 661 5133
🕐 Mon–Sat 9–5.30, Thu 9–8.30, Sun 12–5.30
🍽 Restaurant, café
🚇 Pearse
🚌 Cross-city buses
♿ Very good
💷 Free, except special exhibitions, which are expensive
❓ Public tours Sat 3, Sun 2, 3, 4. Call for lectures

HIGHLIGHTS

● Yeats Archive
● Fra Angelico, *Attempted Martyrdom of SS Cosmas and Damian*
● Titian, *Ecce Homo*
● Vermeer, *Lady Writing*
● Rembrandt, *Rest on the Flight into Egypt*
● Picasso, *Still Life with Mandolin*
● Millennium Wing

National Museum

HIGHLIGHTS

- Prehistoric gold
- Tara Brooch
- Ardagh Chalice
- Cross of Cong
- Tully Lough Cross
- Viking exhibition
- Egyptian room

TIP

- Don't forget many of the treasures of this museum are now on show at Collins Barracks (▷ 48) and worth the 2km (1-mile) trip.

Most of Ireland's greatest treasures are housed in the National Museum. A visit here is a must for a deeper understanding of the country's history and culture since prehistoric times.

Extensive collections For more than a century, the twin institutions of the National Museum (1890) and the National Library have faced each other across the square leading to the Dáil, or Houses of Parliament. On the ground floor, the museum displays western Europe's most extensive collection of prehistoric gold ornaments, mostly dating from the Bronze Age (c1500–500BC). Even more significant are the brooches, chalices, crosses and croziers (AD600–1200), largely the products of Ireland's early Christian monasteries, on show in the Treasury Rooms. Among the greatest gems in

In an attractive leafy location, the National Museum is a wonderful showcase for Ireland's treasures (left)
The beautiful galleried exhibition room of the National Museum features some of the most spectacular prehistoric gold ornaments of the collection

this dazzling collection are the 8th-century Tara Brooch, Ardagh Chalice and the Derrynaflan Hoard. Don't miss the restored rare Tully Lough Cross, an Irish altar cross of the 8th or 9th century. Discovered in Roscommon in fragments, it has been meticulously reconstructed. Also of interest is the 'bog' burial. The body was discovered in 1821 in perfect condition and was dated to 440–200BC. Exposure has now caused severe detoriation.

Tribute Another room on the ground floor is concerned with the Easter Rising of 1916. Be sure not to miss the contrasting exhibitions upstairs on pharaonic Egypt, Viking Dublin and the 2001 Medieval Ireland display spanning the years 1150 to 1550 with displays of sacred reliquaries. A further exhibition traces the 450 years of the story of Irish soldiers, their families and civilians.

THE BASICS

www.museum.ie
✚ H8
✉ Kildare Street
☎ 677 7444
⏰ Tue–Sat 10–5, Sun 2–5
🍴 Café
🚉 Pearse
🚌 Cross-city buses
♿ Ground floor good
🆓 Free
❓ Shop

Natural History Museum

Sketching a fibre-glass hippo (left)
Old bones in a Victorian setting (right)

THE BASICS

www.museum.ie

➕ J8

✉ Merrion Street

☎ 677 7444

🕐 Tue–Sat 10–5, Sun 2–5

🚆 Pearse

🚌 Cross-city buses

♿ Ground floor access only

💷 Free

HIGHLIGHTS

- Giant Irish elk
- Great Irish wolfhound
- Fin whale
- Dodo skeleton
- Hummingbird
- Small meteorite

The old glass cases and creaking floor-boards have changed little since the museum's inauguration in 1857, when Dr. David Livingstone gave the first lecture on his 'African discoveries'.

Fauna The Natural History Museum is one of the four great national institutions flanking the Irish Houses of Parliament. The nucleus of its collection was assembled by the Royal Dublin Society long before it opened, and it has benefited greatly from subsequent gifts. Facing you as you enter is the skeleton of the giant Irish deer, better known as the Irish elk, with its impressive antlers. Beyond is a great array of Irish furred and feathered animals as well as marine species ranging from the greater spotted dogfish and the exotic sunfish to some inpressive giant lobsters.

Dodo The upper floor is given over to animals of the world, among them the great Irish wolf-hound and a massive 20m (66ft) long whale suspended from the ceiling. There is also a skeleton of the flightless dodo and a cluster of hummingbirds. Geology is something of a sideline but is repre-sented by a meteorite that landed in 1810 on County Tipperary in central Ireland and took two hours to cool down. A different kind of curiosity is the outfit worn by Surgeon-Major Thomas Heazle Parke (1858–93), of the Royal Army Medical Corps, who became the first Irishman to cross Africa from coast to coast. The explorer Sir Henry Morton Stanley contributed generously to Parke's statue in front of the museum.

The elegance of a bygone age in the Georgian Number Twenty Nine

Number Twenty Nine

So many of Dublin's 18th-century houses are used as offices that it is a pleasure to see this rare example, perfectly resorted and sumptuously furnished in elegant period style.

The setting Merrion Square epitomizes the graciousness of Georgian Dublin. Three of its four sides are surrounded by four-floor redbrick houses, each elegant doorway crowned by a handsome fanlight. The view from the south side towards St. Stephen's (also known as the Pepper Canister for the shape of its cupola) is one of the city's most attractive streetscapes, and on the southeast corner of the square stands Number Twenty Nine, the only structure in Dublin to preserve the graceful middle-class domesticity of the 18th century.

Nostalgia You enter, as servants did, through the basement, passing the kitchen and pantry (that still has its ingenious rat-proof shelving) to reach the main living quarters on the ground level and parlour floor. Here you will find tasteful Georgian furniture and furnishings, paintings and costumes of the period 1780–1820. The small details are captivating—the hastener (tea trolley) in the kitchen, the feather shaving brush in the gentleman's washing room and the early exercise machine in the bedroom. Climb to the top floor to see the children's playroom, and on the way up admire the wood carving of Napoleon by Bozzanigo Torino in the master bedroom. Don't miss the exquisite Waterford crystal chandelier and the fine Mount Mellick embroidery.

THE BASICS

* J8
* 29 Fitzwilliam Street Lower
* 702 6165
* Tue–Sat 10–5, Sun 2–5. Closed 2 weeks before Christmas
* Tearoom
* Pearse
* 7, 10A, 13A
* None
* Moderate
* Visit by guided tour only

HIGHLIGHTS

* Wood carving of Napoleon
* Examples of Mount Mellick embroidery
* Playroom
* Waterford crystal chandelier

THE SOUTHEAST ★ **TOP 25**

St. Stephen's Green

Newman House
● Apollo Room
● Upper floor salon
● Staircase
● Gerald Manley Hopkins' room

University Church
● Marble panelling
● Carved birds on capitals
● Ceiling
● Golden apse

A hugely popular place when the sun comes out, this park was originally common land used for public hangings, among other activities. Among notable buildings around the green are Newman House and the University Church.

Early days By 1880, St. Stephen's Green had become a public garden, thanks to the benevolence of Lord Ardilaun, a member of the Guinness family. Don't miss the monuments and statues and listen for lunchtime concerts and gigs on the bandstand in summer.

Newman House Named after one of the 19th-century's greatest liberal intellectuals, Newman House is actually two great houses. No. 85 was built in 1738 and the great Lafranchini brothers

The plasterwork by the talented Lafranchini brothers in the Apollo Room, Newman's House, St. Stephen's Green (far left). Enjoying the view (below far left). The Saloon in Newman's House (middle). St. Stephen's Green in full bloom (right). Fountain in St. Stephen's Green (below right)

decorated the walls and ceilings with stucco ornament. Their most notable achievements are the figures of Apollo and the nine muses on the ground floor, and the extravagant ceiling of the Saloon, which stretches the entire length of the upper floor. No. 85 was then bought by Richard Chapel Whaley who went on to build No. 86, embellishing it with fine stucco work. Cardinal Newman used the house in the 1850s and subsequently the house was used by literary greats Gerald Manley Hopkins and James Joyce.

University Church This Byzantine-style church has to be one of Dublin's most unusual ecclesiastical edifices; the only building where Cardinal John Henry Newman left a record of his presence. He built the ornate church on land between No. 86 and No. 87 to promote his ideals.

THE BASICS

Newman House
✚ H8
✉ 85–86 St. Stephen's Green
☎ 716 7422
🕐 Jun–end Aug Tue–Fri tours 12, 2, 3, 4
🍴 Café
🚆 Pearse
🚌 Cross-city buses
♿ None 💷 Moderate

University Church
✚ H8
✉ 87A St. Stephen's Green
☎ 478 1606
🕐 Mon–Sat 9–5.30, Sun 10–1, 5–6
🚌 Cross-city buses
🚆 Pearse
♿ None 💷 Free

HIGHLIGHTS

- Book of Kells
- Book of Durrow
- Book of Armagh

TIPS

- Everyone wants to see the Book of Kells and the best thing is to visit early or come out of season.
- A walking tour in the summer is an informative way to learn more about the college. Ask at the porter's lodge for information.

Stroll around the grounds of the famous college and visit the library where you will find one of the most joyously decorative manuscripts of the first Christian millennium, the Book of Kells.

Surroundings An oasis of fresh air, Trinity College is also the noblest assemblage of classical buildings in the city. Inside, the open square marked with Arnoldo Pomodoro's sculpture *Sphere within Sphere* (1982–83) is surrounded on three sides by some of Dublin's finest modern and ancient buildings—Paul Koralek's New Library (1978) to the south, Benjamin Woodward's splendidly carved Museum building (1853–55) to the east and Thomas Burgh's dignified Old Library (1712–32) to the west. In 1857, Woodward altered Burgh's building and made its

Trinity College, synonomous with learning in Dublin (left). Sphere within a Sphere (1982/3) by Arnaldo Pomodoro in the grounds of the college (below far left). Fellow's Square with the Old Library in the background (below left). Trinity College's famous Old Library, housing Ireland's largest collection of books and the Book of Kells (right)

barrel-vaulted upper floor into one of Ireland's most breathtaking spaces—lined with books from floor to ceiling and decorated with marble busts.

Book of Kells The library is an appropriate setting for Ireland's greatest collection of medieval manuscripts. Among these, pride of place goes to the Book of Kells (c800), a Gospel book that has been bound in four separate sections so that its brilliantly ornamented pages and text may be viewed side by side. Displayed alongside are the important books of Durrow (c700) and Armagh (c800), the latter giving us most of the information we have about Ireland's patron saint, Patrick. The exhibition in the Old Library's main chamber, the Colonnades, called 'Turning Darkness into Light' gives useful background information about the collections.

THE BASICS

www.tcd.ie

✚ H7

✉ College Green

☎ 608 2308

🕐 Old Library: May–end Sep Mon–Sat 9.30–5, Sun 9.30–4.30; Oct–end Apr 12–4.30

🚆 Pearse, Tara Street

🚌 Cross-city buses

♿ Good

🎫 Campus free; Library and Book of Kells expensive

❓ College tours May–end Sep

More to See

DOUGLAS HYDE GALLERY
www.douglashydegallery.com
Contemporary gallery providing talent from Ireland and overseas.
➕ H7 ✉ Trinity College, Nassau Street entrance ☎ 608 1116 🕐 Mon–Fri 11–6, Thu 11–7, Sat 11–4.45 🚉 Pearse 🚌 Cross-city buses ♿ Few 🎟 Free

FITZWILLIAM SQUARE
One of Dublin's most famous Georgian squares, now given over mostly to offices and apartments. Residents have keys to the gardens.
➕ J9 🚌 Cross-city buses 🎟 Free

FUSILIERS' ARCH
Also known as Traitors' Arch, this piece on the northwest corner of St. Stephen's Green is a tribute to the members of the Royal Dublin Fusiliers killed during the Boer War.
➕ H8 ✉ St. Stephen's Green 🚉 Pearse 🚌 Cross-city buses

GAIETY THEATRE
www.gaietytheatre.ie
This attractive theatre, with its landmark Venetian façade, opened on 27th November 1871 with Sir Oliver Goldsmith's *She Stoops to Conquer*, setting the scene for a continuing agenda of high-quality entertainment (▷ 82). In 2003 more than €2 million was invested on a huge restoration project.
➕ H8 ✉ King Street South ☎ 679 5622 🚉 Pearse 🚌 Cross-city buses

IVEAGH GARDENS
One of Dublin's finest yet least well-known parks. Designed in 1863, these secluded gardens shelter a rustic grotto, fountains, maze, archery grounds, wilderness and woodlands.
➕ H9 ✉ Clonmel Street ☎ 475 7816 🕐 Mon–Sat 8–6, Sun 10–6; closes at dusk in winter 🚌 Cross-city buses 🎟 Free

LEINSTER HOUSE
Leinster House is the seat of Irish government and home to Dáil Éireann (House of Representatives) and Senead Éireann (Senate). You can visit by prior arrangement when parliament is not in session.

Ministerial buildings, illuminated by night, flank Leinster House, the seat of the Irish government

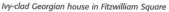

Ivy-clad Georgian house in Fitzwilliam Square

🕂 J8 ✉ Kildare Street ☎ 618 3166
🚇 Pearse 🚌 Cross-city buses ♿ Good
👜 Free

MANSION HOUSE

The official residence of the Lord Mayor of Dublin since 1715. In 1919, the first parliament of the Irish people met here to adopt Ireland's Declaration of Independence from Britain. Closed to visitors.
🕂 H8 ✉ Dawson Street 🚇 Pearse
🚌 Cross-city buses

MERRION SQUARE

The best-preserved Georgian square in Dublin and, as the wall plaques testify, home to many historical Irish figures including Daniel O'Connell and William Butler Yeats. The public park is a hidden gem, take a look after a visit to Number Twenty Nine (▷ 69).
🕂 J8 🚇 Pearse 🚌 Cross-city buses
👜 Free

MOLLY MALONE STATUE

The eponymous fishmonger of song is believed to have lived and worked in Dublin until her death in 1734.
🕂 H7 ✉ Grafton Street Lower 🚇 Pearse
🚌 Cross-city buses

OSCAR WILDE HOUSE

www.amcd.edu
On the north side of Merrion Square is the house where Oscar Wilde lived from 1855 to 1876. It was the first house to be built in the square in 1762 and is an excellent example of Georgian architecture.
🕂 J7 ✉ 1 Merrion Square ☎ 662 0281
🕐 Mon, Wed, Thu tours 10.15, 11.15
🚇 Pearse 🚌 Cross-city buses ♿ No disabled access 👜 Inexpensive

OSCAR WILDE STATUE

This languid life-size figure of the famous writer, reclining on a rock at the northwest corner of Merrion Square, is especially haunting at night.
🕂 J7 ✉ Merrion Square 🚇 Pearse
🚌 Cross-city buses

PATRICK KAVANAGH

Sit and watch the swans slip by with the bronze of poet Patrick Kavanagh

Molly Malone statue in Lower Grafton Street

Dublin City Arms

(1905–67), who loved this piece of leafy calm in the heart of commercial Dublin.

✚ K9 ✉ Grand Canal, near Baggot Street Bridge 🚌 10, 10A

RHA GALLAGHER GALLERY

Prestigious gallery with well-chosen exhibits by Irish and overseas artists. The annual late-spring exhibition showcases the best in contemporary Irish art. Also an attractive outdoor sculpture courtyard.

✚ H8 ✉ 15 Ely Place ☎ 661 2558 🕐 Tue–Sat 11–5, Thu 11–8, Sun 2–5 🚆 Pearse 🚌 Cross-city buses ♿ Good 🖐 Free

ROYAL COLLEGE OF SURGEONS

One of Dublin's later Georgian constructions, this jewel of a building on the northwest corner of St. Stephen's Green, dates from 1806 and was designed by architect Edward Parke. Contact the Admissions Office in advance to arrange a personal tour.

✚ H8 ✉ 123 St. Stephen's Green ☎ 402 2248 🚌 Cross-city buses ♿ Few 🖐 Free

ST. ANN'S CHURCH

Patronized in the 18th century by the new wealthy and influential residents of Georgian Dublin, this 1707 church has a stunning Romanesque façade added in the 1868. For the best view, look down Anne Street South from Grafton Street.

✚ H7 ✉ Dawson Street ☎ 676 7727 🕐 Mon–Fri 10–4 and Sunday service 🚆 Pearse 🚌 Cross-city buses ♿ Good 🖐 Free

WATERWAYS VISITORS CENTRE

Known to locals as 'the box in the docks', the white cube in the middle of the Grand Canal basin houses the Waterways Visitors Centre. With the help of working and scale models, it traces the story of Ireland's inland waterways and their use for commerce and recreation. The museum is central to the ongoing development of the Grand Canal Quay area.

✚ L7 ✉ Grand Canal Quay ☎ 677 7510 🕐 Jun–end Sep daily 9.30–5.30; Oct–end May Wed–Sun 12.30–5 🚆 Grand Canal Dock 🚌 2, 3 🖐 Inexpensive

Royal College of Surgeons

'Faith, Hope and Charity' window in St. Ann's Church

Georgian Dublin Walk

Stroll back in time passing some of the grandest Georgian buildings in Dublin. The squares provide a breath of fresh air in the city.

DISTANCE: 3km (2 miles) **ALLOW:** 2 hours plus stops

START

ST. STEPHEN GREEN NORTH (▷ 70–71)
✚ H8 🚌 Cross-city buses

1 Start at the north side of St. Stephen's Green, (▷ 70–71), by the famous Shelbourne Hotel (▷ 112) close to Kildare Street. Walk down this street.

2 The National Museum of Ireland (▷ 66–67) is on the right-hand side, which houses some of Ireland's greatest treasures. Continue along Kildare Street.

3 On your right you can see the grand buildings of Leinster House (▷ 74), the seat of the Irish government, and beyond the National Library.

4 At the end of the street turn right into Clare Street at the end of which is Merrion Square (▷ 75), one of the finest Georgian squares in the city.

END

ST. STEPHEN'S GREEN SOUTH
(▷ 70–71) ✚ H8 🚌 Cross-city buses

8 At the end of the street turn right into Leeson Street Lower and keep going until you reach the south edge of St. Stephen's Green.

7 Continue into Fitwilliam Street Upper to Fitzwilliam Square and turn right along its southern edge. Some of the best houses are here—take a note of the attractive doors and fanlights above. Turn left at the end of the square into Pembroke Street Upper.

6 Walk along Merrion Square West and left into Merrion Square South. At the end is Number Twenty Nine (▷ 69), a gracious Georgian townhouse. Turn right along Fitzwilliam Street Lower.

5 Turn right here—across the road is the Oscar Wilde House (▷ 75).

Shopping

ALIAS TOM
One of Dublin's longest-standing men's stores. Paul Smith, Versace, Issay Miyake, Donna Karan, Calvin Klein, Hugo Boss, Yves St. Laurent and many, many more.
✚ H7 ✉ Duke Lane
☎ 671 5443 🚉 Pearse
🚌 Cross-city buses

APOLLO GALLERY
www.apollogallery.ie
The specialists in Irish art. Patrons include movie star Sylvester Stallone, former Formula One racing team owner Eddie Jordan, Microsoft USA and Sky TV.
✚ H7 ✉ 51c Dawson Street
☎ 671 2609 🚉 Pearse
🚌 Cross-city buses

AVOCA
www.avoca.ie
One of Ireland's oldest surviving businesses, founded in 1723 and fast emerging as a fine department store for unique and exclusive high quality items combining the traditional with the fashionable. The splendid food hall is packed with Irish delicacies including preserves, oils and biscuits all under the Avoca label. Freshly baked foods, too.
✚ H7 ✉ 11–13 Suffolk Street ☎ 677 4215 🚉 Pearse
🚌 Cross-city buses

A WEAR
Fashionable clothes for young women, with reassuring price tags, Ireland's own main street chain

store offers plenty by way of choice. Stock changes every two weeks.
✚ H7 ✉ Grafton Street and other branches ☎ 671 7200
🚉 Pearse 🚌 Cross-city buses

BLARNEY WOOLLEN MILLS
www.blarney.com
An amazing collection of sweaters, woollen rugs, and throws, Irish tweeds and linen, alongside great names like Waterford Crystal, Belleek, Royal Tara and Irish Dresden.
✚ H7 ✉ 21–23 Nassau Street ☎ 451 6111 🚉 Pearse
🚌 Cross-city buses

BROWN THOMAS
www.brownthomas.com
Ireland's stylish department store showcases Irish and international designer clothes. Also household furnishings, cosmetics, leather goods,

MADE IN IRELAND
If you're looking for something of modern Ireland for your home, check out the following:
Jerpoint glass—heavy, hand-blown pieces of simple design with colour bursts. John Rocha has brought Waterford crystal up-to-date with a designer line that is minimalist. Nicholas Mosse's sponged pottery is very popular. Louis Mulcahy is one of Ireland's most prolific ceramicists. Great designs.

accessories and linens.
✚ H7 ✉ Grafton Street
☎ 605 6666 🚉 Pearse
🚌 Cross-city buses

BT2
www.brownthomas.com
Brown Thomas' trendy younger sibling sells more casual clothes like DKNY, French Connection and Full Circle. Wonderful views of Grafton Street.
✚ H7 ✉ Grafton Street
☎ 605 6666, ext. 1200
🚉 Pearse 🚌 Cross-city buses

BUTLER'S CHOCOLATE CAFÉ
www.butlerschocolates.com
Mouth-watering selection of Irish handmade chocolates from the original Mrs Bailey-Butler's recipe of 1932. Go on treat yourself.
✚ H7 ✉ 51A Grafton Street
☎ 671 0599 🚉 Pearse
🚌 Cross-city buses

CATHACH BOOKS
www.rarebooks.ie
Dublin's leading rare and antiquarian bookshop, specializing in books of Irish interest with a particular emphasis on 20th-century literature.
✚ H7 ✉ 10 Duke Street
☎ 671 5120 🚉 Pearse
🚌 Cross-city buses

CELTIC NOTE
www.celticnote.ie
One of the country's best specialist Irish music stores has everything from classical to traditional, rock to contemporary.

✚ H7 ✉ Nassau Street
☎ 670 4157 🚊 Pearse
🚌 Cross-city buses

CHARLES BYRNE

Established in 1870, Charles Byrne are renowned for their expertize in stringed instruments and stock Ireland's best range of *bodhráns*, handmade by experts.
✚ G7 ✉ 21–22 Stephen's Street Lower ☎ 478 1904 🚊 Pearse 🚌 Cross-city buses

CELTIC WHISKEY SHOP

www.celticwhiskeyshop.com
Tempting selection of Irish whiskies, chocolates, liquers and wines. Boasts one of the best ranges of whiskies in the city.
✚ H7 ✉ 27–28 Dawson Street ☎ 675 9744 🚊 Pearse 🚌 Cross-city buses

CLEO

If handknit sweaters, tweedy skirts and high-end country style is your style, Cleo's is the place for you. Run by the Joyce family since 1936, Cleo's specialize in natural fibre clothes made in knitters' and weavers' homes.
✚ H8 ✉ 18 Kildare Street ☎ 676 1421 🚊 Pearse 🚌 Cross-city buses

THE DECENT CIGAR EMPORIUM

www.decent-cigar.com
All you would want to know and what to buy concerning the ultimate in cigars. Buy just one or boxes of them.
✚ H7 ✉ 46 Grafton Street ☎ 671 6451 🚊 Pearse 🚌 Cross-city buses

THE DRAWING ROOM

Ornate mahogany frames, embroidered cushions and richly decorated lampstands made from Chinese procelain. Expensive.
✚ H7 ✉ 29 Westbury Mall, off Grafton Street ☎ 677 2083 🚊 Pearse 🚌 Cross-city buses

GREENE'S BOOK-SHOP

www.greenesbookshop.com
Many famous literary names have browsed in this shop, which has been in business since 1843. Second-hand and Irish books, plus rare editions.

TRADITION LIVES ON

Irish traditional music is played in pubs all over the city every night of the week and is generally free. Music is often spontaneous, with musicians joining in an impromptu *seisún* (session). The Irish have grown up with this music; it has been handed down through the generations and instruments are learned instinctively by watching others. All the traditional instruments and sheet music can be found in the excellent music shops to be found in the city.

✚ H7 ✉ 16 Clare Street
☎ 676 2554 🚊 Pearse
🚌 Cross-city buses

HMV

This is the biggest music store in the city with every type of music—pop, rock, folk, classical and even a section selling vinyl. Also videos, DVDs and video games.
✚ H7 ✉ 65 Grafton Street ☎ 679 5334 🚊 Pearse 🚌 Cross-city buses

HODGES & FIGGIS

This famous old bookstore was established in 1768 and is particularly revered for its collection of works on Celtic and Irish history, culture, art and literature. It has excellent ordering facilities. There is also a great coffee shop on the first floor.
✚ H7 ✉ 56–58 Dawson Street ☎ 677 4754 🚊 Pearse 🚌 Cross-city buses

HOUSE OF IRELAND

www.houseofireland.com
Traditional Irish fashion, crafts, Waterford crystal, Belleek china and Aran knitwear. Also the less well-known Galway Crystal.
✚ H7 ✉ 38 Nassau Street ☎ 671 1111 🚊 Pearse 🚌 Cross-city buses

IB JORGENSEN FINE ART

www.jorgensenfineart.com
Ireland's most popular fashion designer turned to fine art in 1992 and

hasn't looked back. Prepare to pay top prices for works by Jack Yeats, Frederick Osborne and Mary Swanzy. Also solo exhibitions of international contemporary artists.
✚ H7 ✉ 29 Molesworth Street ☎ 661 9758 🚉 Pearse 🚌 Cross-city buses

KERLIN GALLERY
www.kerlin.ie
This is arguably Dublin's leading contemporary art gallery, established in 1988, showcasing the work of top artists like Dorothy Cross, Feilim Egan, David Godbold and Paul Seawright.
✚ H7 ✉ Anne's Lane, off Anne Street South ☎ 670 9093 🚉 Pearse 🚌 Cross-city buses

KEVIN AND HOWLIN
www.kelvinandhowlin.com
Shop here for your Donegal tweeds. All the usual hardwearing items—jackets, waistcoats, hats and ties in both modern and traditional styles. They last for years.
✚ H7 ✉ 31 Nassau Street ☎ 677 0257 🚉 Pearse 🚌 Cross-city buses

KILKENNY CENTRE
An essential stopping point for stylish Irish decorative objects for the home, glass, books, fashion and jewellery—traditional but creative.
✚ H7 ✉ 6 Nassau Street ☎ 677 7066 🚉 Pearse 🚌 Cross-city buses

KNOBS AND KNOCKERS
www.knobsandknockers.ie
Everything you could think of to furnish your door. The Irish Claddagh knocker, based on the symbolic 'friendship, loyalty and love' Claddagh ring, is one of the most popular lines.
✚ H7 ✉ 19 Nassau Street ☎ 671 0288 🚉 Pearse 🚌 Cross-city buses

LEMON STREET GALLERY
www.lemonstreet.com
This gallery offers an intimidation-free zone to those wishing to look at framed and unframed work by a wide range of Irish and international artists.
✚ H7 ✉ Lemon Street, off Grafton Street ☎ 671 0244 🚉 Pearse 🚌 Cross-city buses

WHAT'S YOUR STYLE

There are some great shops in Dublin displaying a wide range of home interior products, many produced by Irish craftspeople and also by fashion designers turning to objects and furniture. Interior design is popular worldwide, and Dublin is gaining more shops for the enthusiast. Beautiful items in stone, wood, glass and other natural materials can be bought in both traditional and contemporary styles. Terence Conran, John Rocha and other well-known names.

L. M. RUBAN
Amazing selection of ribbons, cords, braids, fringing and tassels in a myriad of widths and a rainbow of hues.
✚ H7 ✉ 19 Westbury Mall, off Grafton Street ☎ 677 0791 🚉 Pearse 🚌 Cross-city buses

LOUIS COPELAND
www.louiscopeland.com
A Louis Copeland suit, made-to-measure or off the peg, is a rite of passage for well-dressed Irish men. Chosen by politicians and society figures.
✚ J8 ✉ 30 Pembroke Street Lower ☎ 661 0111 🚌 10

LOUIS MULCAHY
Hand-thrown pots, teapots, vases and other ceramics. Also stunning hand-woven wall hangings.
✚ H7 ✉ 46 Dawson Street ☎ 670 9311 🚉 Pearse 🚌 Cross-city buses

LOUISE KENNEDY
Kennedy's tasteful, exclusive clothing and crystal collections are sold alongside luxury branded accessories and gorgeous gifts to take home.
✚ J8 ✉ 56 Merrion Square ☎ 419 1810 🚉 Pearse 🚌 Cross-city buses

MAGILLS
Salami, meats, bread, cheese, coffee, herbs, spices and every sort of packaged delicacy.
✚ H7 ✉ 14 Clarendon Street ☎ 671 3830 🚉 Pearse 🚌 Cross-city buses

MCCULLOUGH PIGOTT

Highly respected by music lovers who while away the time gazing at the musical instruments and browsing through the sheet music.

H7 25 Suffolk Street 671 2410 Pearse Cross-city buses

MARKS & SPENCER

It is the famous high street store selling all its usual men's, women's, and children's ranges and homeware. But you might not recognize it at first–not in its corporate hues, this branch is in a lovely building decorated in black and red.

H7 15–20 Grafton Street 679 7855 Pearse Cross-city buses

MITCHELL & SON WINE MERCHANTS

www.mitchellandson.com

Dublin's oldest and possibly finest wine merchants stocks interesting and exclusive vintages.

H8 21 Kildare Street 676 0766 Pearse Cross-city buses

POWERSCOURT TOWNHOUSE CENTRE

www.powerscourt.com

A warren of boutiques, gift and craft stores, restaurants, cafés and art galleries within a converted Georgian town house. The Design Centre is well worth a look. Good place for a coffee break.

H7 Clarendon Street 671 7000 Pearse Cross-city buses

ST. STEPHEN'S GREEN CENTRE

www.stephensgreen.com

A light, airy complex over three floors with good parking. The mall combines more expensive specialist shops with Dunnes department store and bargain emporia.

H8 Grafton Street 478 0888 Pearse Cross-city buses

SHERIDANS CHEESE SHOP

This glorious shop packed with massive blocks of cheese is a wonderful showcase for Irish farmhouse varieties that are winning awards worldwide. Also Irish foods such as salmon, and jams and marmalades.

H8 11 Anne Street South 679 3143 Pearse Cross-city buses

TRINITY CRAFT CENTRE

Inspiring potters, jewellers and textile designers work and sell in around 35 small workshops here. Look for pieces by quirky silversmith Alan Ardiff and scarves by Mel Bradly (who also works for John Rocha and Louise Kennedy).

K7 Pearse Street 677 5655 Pearse 13

SILVER SHOP

Wide range of antique silver and silver-plate from the conventional to the unusual Irish portrait miniatures. Prices start low and head up into the thousands.

H7 First Floor, Powerscourt Townhouse Centre, Clarendon Street 679 4147 Pearse Cross-city buses

STOCK

Furniture, fabrics, rugs, lighting and an impressive range of kitchen utensils and cookware. Serious cooks will come across more unusual items at Stock that are hard to find elsewhere.

H8 33–34 King Street South 679 4316 Pearse Cross-city buses

SUSAN HUNTER

www.susanhunterlingerie.ie

Tiny but exclusive lingerie store. Ireland's only source of La Perla and Tuttabankem. Pricey but irresistable.

H7 13 Westbury Mall, off Grafton Street 679 1271 Pearse Cross-city buses

TRIBE

A special shop for Ireland's urban skaters and surfers, Karl Swan's laid-back store is crammed with well-chosen casual clothes, shoes and accessories.

H8 First floor, St. Stephen's Green Centre 475 0311 Pearse Cross-city buses

Entertainment and Nightlife

ENTERTAINMENT AND NIGHTLIFE

THE SOUTHEAST

CAFÉ EN SEINE
The beautiful interior of this long bar has strikingly high ceilings supporting French bistro lighting. The relaxed daytime atmosphere hots up in the evening when the bar fills out with office workers.
✚ H7 ✉ 40 Dawson Street
☎ 677 4369 🚆 Pearse
🚌 Cross-city buses

CAPTAIN AMERICA'S COOKHOUSE AND BAR
www.captainamericas.com
This is a lively American-style bar and diner that was established here in 1971. Since then it has amassed a huge collection of rock and roll memorabilia. It also claims to be the only fully licensed bar that's actually on Grafton Street, and offers a great line in cocktails. Be prepared for crowds—especially on Saturday.
✚ H7 ✉ 44 Grafton Street
☎ 671 5266 🚆 Pearse
🚌 Cross-city buses

THE CHOCOLATE BAR
Hot and cold designer sandwiches by day for trendies and office workers; a popular haunt by night. Great cocktails.
✚ G9 ✉ Old Harcourt Station 35 Harcourt Street (inside POD nightspot) ☎ 478 0166 🕐 Food served at lunch only 🚌 Cross-city buses

DOHENY AND NESBITT
A distinguished old pub away from the usual tourist drinking spots, it attracts politicians and media people to its three floors and bars well-stocked wtih whiskies and stouts. Mirrored walls, high ceilings and intimate snugs betray its Victoria origins, over 130 years ago.
✚ J8 ✉ 5 Baggot Street Lower ☎ 676 2945 🚌 10, 15X, 25X, 49X

FOCUS THEATRE
This tiny space has seen many surprises and excellent performances. Movie star Gabriel Byrne was once a regular.
✚ J8 ✉ 6 Pembroke Place, off Pembroke Street ☎ 676 3071 🚆 Pearse 🚌 10

GAIETY THEATRE
www.gaietytheatre.com
An integral part of Dublin theatreland, with a varied agenda of opera,

---

TOP TALENT

You would expect the capital of literary Ireland to be overflowing with theatrical talent—and you would be right. *Riverdance* and *Dancing at Lughnasa* both played to Irish audiences before receiving global acclaim, and Martin McDonaugh packed Dubliners in to see his Lenane trilogy prior to winning several Tony awards on Broadway. In contrast, the annual Christmas pantomimes see Irish celebrities ham up traditional tales.

---

musicals, classic plays, comedies, pantomime and touring shows. After the curtain goes down on Friday and Saturday, the theatre transforms into a salsa and soul nightclub.
✚ H8 ✉ King Street South
☎ 677 1717 🚆 Pearse
🚌 Cross-city buses

INTERNATIONAL BAR
Indulge in a hefty helping of Irish wit at the home of the Comedy Cellar, founded by comic geniuses Ardal O'Hanlon, Dylan Moran and others. The daily evening schedule of events encompasses blues and country music as well as comedy.
✚ H7 ✉ 23 Wicklow Street
☎ 677 9250 🚆 Pearse
🚌 Cross-city buses

LILLIE'S BORDELLO
A home-away-from-home for pop and movie stars. House, chart and oldie music.
✚ H7 ✉ Adam Court, Grafton Street ☎ 679 9204
🚆 Pearse 🚌 Cross-city buses

MCDAID'S
A Dublin literary institution, it was here that the likes of Brendan Behan, Patrick Kavanagh and Flann O'Brien used as their local. Does get crowded but the atmosphere is great, with its wood and stained glass.
✚ H7 ✉ 3 Harry Street
☎ 679 4395 🚆 Pearse
🚌 Cross-city buses

MESSRS MAGUIRE

If you fancy a change from Guinness try the excellent beers brewed in the basement at this popular labyrinth of bars and cosy snugs. Live music and good food.

➕ H6 ✉ 1–2 Burgh Quay
☎ 670 5777 🚆 Tara Street
🚌 Cross-city buses

MULLIGANS

www.mulligans.ie
A pub since 1820, Mulligans is a Guinness drinker's institution. Retaining its Victorian mahogany furnishings, it has resisted change.

➕ H6 ✉ 8 Poolbeg Street
☎ 677 5582 🚆 Tara Street
🚌 Cross-city buses

NATIONAL CONCERT HALL

www.ncl.ie.com
Busy Georgian concert hall with a modern 250-seat auditorium and world-class acoustics that is home to the RTé National Symphony Orchestra. Top artists perform here.

➕ H9 ✉ Earlsfort Terrace
☎ 417 0000 🚆 Pearse
🚌 10, 11, 14, 15,44, 46, 86

O'DONAGHUE'S

www.odonaghues.ie
Renowned for its associations with the famous folk group the Dubliners, this is a good place for impromptu sessions but it does get crowded.

➕ J8 ✉ 15 Merrion Row
☎ 676 2807 🚆 Pearse
🚌 Cross-city buses

O'NEILLS

www.oneillsdublin.com
O'Neills always offers a friendly welcome. It is renowned for its ageless character and numerous alcoves and snugs. Good for the *craic* and some tasty food.

➕ J7 ✉ 36–37 Pearse Street
☎ 679 3656 🚆 Pearse
🚌 Cross-city buses

POD

www.pod.ie
The Place of Dance is one of the hippest clubs in town. Tight door policy restricts entry to the stylish and sober. Different club each evening but a good mix of happy house and popular dance floor hits.

➕ G9 ✉ Old Harcourt Station, 35 Harcourt Street ☎ 478 0166
🚌 Cross-city buses

🎵

THE CLASSICS

Dublin has a thriving classical music and opera scene, though performances are irregular. The National Concert Hall stages a full schedule but other venues offer seasonal performances only. The Gaiety Theatre plays host to Dublin's most professional and prolific opera society. To find out about forthcoming events, call the box offices direct or check the listings in the Irish Times. Reservations are recommended for most performances.

THE RED BOX

www.pod.ie
In the same building as POD (▷ this page), this was the venue where Westlife held some of their finest rehearsals. It is still a popular dance venue.

➕ G9 ✉ Old Harcourt Station, 35 Harcourt Street
☎ 478 0225 🚆 Pearse
🚌 Cross-city buses

RENARDS

www.renards.ie
Late-night club with busy basement dance floor (members only), a café/bar and an upstairs VIP area populated by thirty-somethings from the worlds of fashion, media and film.

➕ H7 ✉ 33–35 Frederick Street South ☎ 677 5876
🚆 Pearse 🚌 Cross-city buses

SCREEN

Fringe and mainstream movies on three screens. Good discounts on matinees. Bring your own munchies—the selection here isn't good.

➕ H6 ✉ D'Olier Street
☎ 672 5500 🚆 Pearse
🚌 Cross-city buses

THE SUGAR CLUB

www.thesugarclub.ie
Park of the new wave of cocktail bars, located in a converted cinema. Swing, jazz, salsa and blues hit the mark.

➕ H9 ✉ 8 Leeson Street Lower ☎ 678 7188 🚆 Pearse
🚌 10, 11, 14, 15,44, 46, 86

THE DESIGN CENTRE

Restaurants

THE SOUTHEAST

RESTAURANTS

PRICES

Prices are approximate, based on a 3-course meal for one person.

€€€	over €40
€€	€20–€40
€	under €20

ALPHA RESTAURANT (€)

Traditional café that serves all-day breakfast as well as huge mixed grills and snacks. Terrific place to recover from the morning after the night before.

➕ H7 ✉ Corner Wicklow Street and Clarendon Street ☎ 677 0213 🕐 Breakfast, lunch and dinner daily 🚉 Pearse 🚌 Cross-city buses

AYA (€€)

Dublin's hippest, fun conveyor sushi bar and restaurant, just off Grafton Street. One of the many different types of cuisine to hit the Dublin restaurant scene.

➕ H7 ✉ Clarendon Street ☎ 677 1544 🕐 Lunch and dinner daily 🚉 Pearse 🚌 Cross-city buses

BANG CAFÉ (€€)

Cool and minimal, Bang is as trendy and fresh as its get-ahead clientele. The eclectic, modern menu is as fashionable as its cosmopolitan interiors. Modern European menu.

➕ J8 ✉ Merrion Row ☎ 676 0898 🕐 Lunch, dinner Mon–Sat 🚉 Pearse 🚌 Cross-city buses

BEWLEY'S ORIENTAL CAFÉ (€)

www.bewleys.com
When Bewleys reopened in 2005 under new management it was with a sigh of relief that they retained the glorious wood-panel rooms and stained-glass windows. Steeped in history and nostalgia it includes the fish restaurant, Mackerel, the Cafe Bar Deli and the Mezzanine Café & Bar. The Café Theatre lunchtime drama and literary readings, and evening cabaret, are regular events.

➕ H7 ✉ 78 Grafton Street ☎ 672 7719 🕐 Mackerel: Mon–Sat 12–4, 5–10, Sun brunch 12–4; Mezz Cafe: daily 8am–10.30/11pm; Cafe Bar Deli: Thu–Sat 12–11, Sun–Wed 12–10; Café Theatre call for details 🚉 Pearse 🚌 Cross-city buses

TIPS FOR EATING OUT

Eating out is extremely popular in Dublin, so reserve ahead. Some restaurants close on Monday.
Most serious restaurants offer a fixed-price lunch menu that represents excellent value. 'Earlybird' meals are popular, a value meal usually served before 7pm. A service charge of 12.5 per cent is generally added and many diners add a tip of about 5 to 10 per cent of the bill. If service is not included, a tip of 12.5–15 per cent is usual.

BROWNES RESTAURANT (€€€)

www.brownesdublin.com
One of Dublin's most sophisticated and stylish restaurants housed in a Georgian townhouse hotel on St. Stephen's Green. Eat continental cuisine in a spectacular dining room.

➕ H8 ✉ 22 St. Stephen's Green ☎ 638 3939 🕐 Lunch Sun–Fri, dinner daily 🚌 Cross-city buses

BT2 (€)

www.brownthomas.com
Glass-fronted café in the BT2 store with great views of Grafton Street. Sit in white minimalist splendour nibbling tasty sandwiches, pastries and salads or sip frothy coffees, hot chocolate or juices.

➕ H7 ✉ Grafton Street ☎ 679 5666 ext. 1200 🕐 Breakfast, lunch and snacks 🚉 Pearse 🚌 Cross-city buses

CAFÉ FRESH (€)

www.cafe-fresh.com
An addition to Dublin's vegetarian scene offering healthy, nutritious and appealing options while maintaining taste. From hot dishes sandwiches and juices. Lots of organic produce. Perfect after a morning's shopping.

➕ H7 ✉ 1 Top Floor, Powerscourt Townhouse Centre, William Street South ☎ 671 9669 🕐 Breakfast and lunch daily 🚉 Pearse 🚌 Cross-city buses

CAFÉ JAVA (€)

Plenty for all tastes and appetites at this popular breakfast haunt, which can be busy.

H7 5 Anne Street South 660 0675 Breakfast and lunch daily Pearse 11, 11A, 11B, 13, 46A, and cross-city buses

CHILI CLUB (€€)

Small Thai restaurant selling tasty food.

H7 1 Anne's Lane, off South Anne's Street 677 3721 Lunch Mon–Sat, dinner daily Pearse Cross-city buses

CHOMPYS (€)

Chompys is popular for its great American breakfast and brunch cooked to order and eaten on the balcony.

H7 Powerscourt Shopping Centre, William Street South 679 4552 Closes 5.30pm Mon–Sat Pearse Cross-city buses

COCOON (€)

Modern, chic and sleek, this hotel bar serves champagne and fries in equal quantities to Dublin's smart set.

H7 Royal Hibernian Way, Dawson Street 679 6259 Food served at lunch only Pearse Cross-city buses

CORNUCOPIA (€)

Long-established city-centre vegetarian restaurant and shop with optional takeout service.

H7 19 Wicklow Street 677 7583 Breakfast, lunch and dinner Mon–Sat (closes 7pm Sun) Pearse Cross-city buses

DIEP LE SHAKER (€)

www.diep.net

A stylish haunt offering some of the best, beautifully presented Thai cuisine in Ireland. Sophisticated surroundings with a vibrant atmosphere.

J8 55 Pembroke Lane 661 1829 Lunch Mon–Fri, dinner Mon–Sat Lansdowne Road Cross-city buses

EASTERN BALTI HOUSE (€€)

Well known for its range of authentic dishes.

H7 34–35 William Street South 671 0506

PUB GRUB

Pubs in Dublin are synonymous with drinking, Guinness, traditional Irish music and good *craic*. But pub food is becoming increasingly popular and, particularly for those on a limited budget, good value. You can get some excellent hearty meals, including traditional Irish stews, the boxty (potato pancake) and colcannon (cabbage and potato). There is often a carvery with a choice of salads. Sample any of these accompanied by a pint of Guinness to be like a local.

Lunch Mon–Sat, dinner daily Pearse Cross-city buses

L'ECRIVAIN (€€€)

www.lecrivain.com

Chef Derry Clarke's popular Irish restaurant continues to grow in stature. It is well known for its fresh fish, which is caught all over Ireland on the same day. Friendly service.

J8 109a Lower Baggot Street 661 1919 Lunch Mon–Fri, dinner Mon–Sat 10

EDDIE ROCKETS (€)

www.edddierockets.ie

US-style diner offering burgers, fries, hot dogs, buffalo wings and shakes. Open from breakfast until midnight during the week, until late Thu–Sat.

H7 7 South Anne Street 679 7340 Lunch and dinner daily Pearse Cross-city buses

EXPRESSO BAR (€)

Matte black-and-chrome upscale café. Fashionable food, delicate pastries and herbal teas.

K9 St. Mary's Road 660 0585 Breakfast, lunch and dinner Tue–Sat, (closes 6pm Mon, Sun) Lansdowne Road 5, 7A, 45

FIRE (€€€)

www.mansionhouse.ie/fire

The spacious dining room is set in the resplendent bell epoque era. A modern European menu with

a twist. Special 'jazz' brunch on Saturdays.
✚ H8 ✉ The Mansion House, Dawson Street ☎ 676 7200 ⊙ Brunch Sat, dinner Mon–Sat 🚌 Cross-city buses

FITZERS (€€)
www.fitzers.ie
The most fashionable branch of the popular chain. Busy, fiery Mediterranean menu plus chunky burgers and fries.
✚ H8 ✉ 51 Dawson Street ☎ 677 1155 ⊙ Lunch and dinner daily 🚇 Pearse 🚌 Cross-city buses

IMPERIAL (€)
A family-run business established in Dublin since 1985, with some of the best Chinese cooking in the city.
✚ H7 ✉ 13 Wicklow Street ☎ 677 2580 ⊙ Lunch and dinner daily 🚇 Pearse 🚌 Cross-city buses

JACOB'S LADDER (€€–€€€)
www.jacobsladder.ie
This light and airy restaurant spreads over two floors with great views of Trinity College. Well balanced modern cooking, using seasonal ingredients and offering some good vegetarian options.
✚ H7 ✉ 4 Nassau Street ☎ 670 3865 ⊙ Lunch and dinner Tue–Sat 🚇 Pearse 🚌 Cross-city buses

KAFFE MOCKA (€)
Fifty types of coffee and an extensive menu of sandwiches, snacks

and tasty mains. Also, board games, newspapers and a library upstairs.
✚ H7 ✉ 39 William Street South ☎ 671 0978 ⊙ Breakfast, lunch and dinner daily 🚇 Pearse 🚌 Cross-city buses

KEOGHS (€)
Great for snacks, paninis and food to take out. Nice range of coffees and refreshing freshly squeezed orange juice.
✚ H7 ✉ 1–2 Trinity Street ☎ 677 8599 ⊙ Daily 🚇 Pearse 🚌 Cross-city buses

LANGKAWI (€€)
Excellent Malaysian restaurant with an exciting, extensive menu. Totally delicious food that's high on taste.
✚ K9 ✉ 46 Baggot Street Upper ☎ 668 2760 ⊙ Lunch Mon–Fri, dinner

daily 🚇 Lansdowne Road 🚌 10

LANYONS (€€€)
www.ocallaghanhotels.com
Excellent service and lavish surroundings ensure a memorable dining experience. The contemporary Irish cooking combines fine traditional dishes with exciting new trends.
✚ J8 ✉ The Davenport Hotel, Merrion Square ☎ 607 3500 ⊙ Lunch Mon–Fri, dinner daily 🚇 Pearse 🚌 Cross-city buses

LONGCHAMP @ NO. 10 (€€€)
www.longfields.ie
Fine dining in elegant surroundings can be found at this restaurant in Longfields hotel (▷ 111). It has its own separate entrance and is open to nonresidents. Head chef Alan Devlin ensures a first-rate modern Irish menu.
✚ J8 🚌 10 Fitzwilliam Street Lower ☎ 676 1060 ⊙ Breakfast, lunch and dinner 🚇 Pearse 🚌 Cross-city buses

MAO (€€)
www.cafemao.com
Modern food and Warholesque lithographs. No reservations, but tables turn quickly.
✚ H7 ✉ 2–3 Chatham Row ☎ 670 4899 ⊙ Lunch and dinner daily 🚇 Pearse 🚌 Cross-city buses

LA MÈRE ZOU (€€)
www.lamerezou.ie
Contemporary eatery that prides itself on good

Franco-Belgian cuisine. Ask about the good value 'Big Plates'.

⊞ H8 ⊠ 22 St. Stephen's Green ☎ 661 6669 🕐 Lunch Mon–Fri, dinner daily 🚇 Pearse 🚌 Cross-city buses

NUDE (€)

Healthy fast food with an organic slant and the most creative of wraps, salads and smoothies.

⊞ H7 ⊠ 21 Suffolk Street ☎ 677 5577 🕐 Breakfast, lunch and dinner daily (closes 7pm Sun) 🚇 Pearse 🚌 Cross-city buses

OCEAN (€–€€)

Glass surrounded bar and restaurant with wonderful waterside view. The menu offers delicate portions of fresh shellfish and seafood along with wraps and salads. Perfect setting for sunny summer lunches.

⊞ L7 ⊠ Grand Canal Basin, Ringsend Road ☎ 668 8862 🕐 Lunch, dinner Mon–Sun 🚇 Grand Canal Dock 🚌 3

ONE PICO (€€–€€€)

www.onepico.com
In a delightful warm and relaxed ambience, the first-class cooking at One Pico makes the most of local produce such as Irish Angus beef. Special tasting menus give you an insight into the cuisine.

⊞ H8 ⊠ 5–6 Molesworth Place, School House Lane ☎ 676 0300 🕐 Lunch, dinner Mon–Sun 🚇 Pearse 🚌 Cross-city buses

PASTA FRESCA (€)

A constantly fast-moving haunt dishing up excellent pasta and pizzas served until late.

⊞ H7 ⊠ 3–4 Chatham Street ☎ 679 2402 🕐 Lunch and dinner daily 🚇 Pearse 🚌 Cross-city buses

RAJDOOT TANDOORI (€€€)

Honest, dependable North Indian food. Excellent service from the friendly staff.

⊞ H7 ⊠ Westbury Hotel, Clarendon Street ☎ 679 4280 🕐 Lunch Mon–Sat, dinner daily 🚇 Pearse 🚌 Cross-city buses

RESTAURANT PATRICK GUILBAUD (€€€)

www.themerrionhotel.com
Superlative cuisine by French chef Patrick Guilbaud. Desserts to die for. Tastefully decorated, with a wonderful collection of Irish art.

RAISING A GLASS

The Irish have a reputation for enjoying a tipple and it's not surprising given the quality of their native drinks. So try a drop of the following: For stout sample Guinness or Murphy's. For whiskey–a traditional chaser to your stout–there's Jamesons or Busmills. And don't forget the Baileys, made from two of Ireland's finest products– whiskey and cream.

⊞ J8 ⊠ Merrion Hotel, 21 Merrion Street Upper ☎ 676 4192 🕐 Lunch and dinner Tue–Sat 🚇 Pearse 🚌 Cross-city buses

STEPS OF ROME (€)

Divine pizza by the slice plus other gutsy Italian fare.

⊞ H7 ⊠ Chatham Street ☎ 670 5630 🕐 Lunch and dinner daily 🚇 Pearse 🚌 Cross-city buses

THE TERRACE LOUNGE (€)

www.jurys-dublin-hotels.com
Located in the Westbury Hotel, this is the perfect place for afternoon tea with a wonderful panoramic view of Dublin. Relax and watch the world go round.

⊞ H7 ⊠ Grafton Street ☎ 679 1122 🕐 Afternoon tea 3pm–5.30pm 🚇 Pearse 🚌 Cross-city buses

TRENTUNO (€€)

Bright modern restaurant offering huge portions of well-known Italian fare.

⊞ H7 ⊠ 31 Wicklow Street ☎ 677 4190 🕐 Lunch and dinner daily 🚇 Pearse 🚌 Cross-city buses

WAGAMAMA (€€)

www.wagamama.ie
Fast and furious woks churn out healthy substantial Japanese dishes in minimalist surroundings.

⊞ H8 ⊠ St. Stephen's Green Shopping Centre, South King Street ☎ 478 2152 🕐 Lunch and dinner daily 🚇 Pearse 🚌 Cross-city buses

Just a short distance outside Dublin the beautiful Irish countryside is a delight with pretty seaside villages, stunning lakes and ancient Celtic burial sites. A trip to the suburbs can also be rewarding.

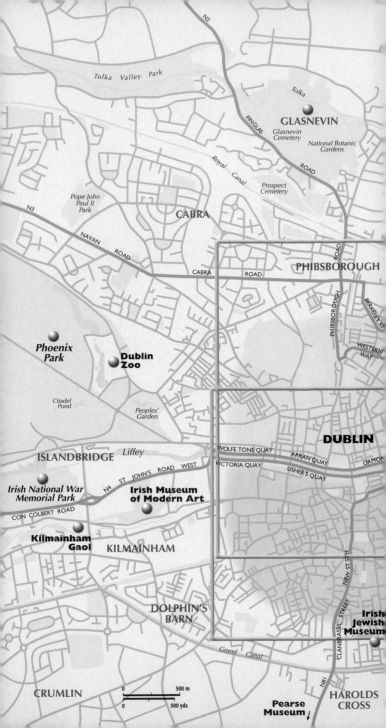

N2

Tolka Valley Park

Tolka

FINGLAS

GLASNEVIN

Glasnevin
Cemetery

National Botanic
Gardens

Royal Canal

ROAD

Prospect
Cemetery

Pope John
Paul II
Park

N3

CABRA

NAVAN ROAD

PHIBSBOROUGH

CABRA ROAD

PHIBSBOROUGH ROAD

BERKELEY ROAD

WESTERN WAY

Phoenix
Park

Dublin
Zoo

Citadel
Pond

Peoples'
Garden

Liffey

DUBLIN

ISLANDBRIDGE

WOLFE TONE QUAY

ARRAN QUAY

ORMON

ST. JOHN'S ROAD WEST

VICTORIA QUAY

USHER'S QUAY

Irish National War
Memorial Park

N4

Irish Museum
of Modern Art

CON COLBERT ROAD

Kilmainham
Gaol

KILMAINHAM

NEW ST. STH

DOLPHIN'S
BARN

CLANBRASSIL STREET

Irish
Jewish
Museum

Grand Canal

CRUMLIN

0   500 m

0   500 yds

Pearse
Museum

N81

HAROLDS
CROSS

Casino, Marino

The south facing façade of the striking Casino at Marino, with its impressive columns

THE BASICS

✚ M1
✉ Off the Malahide Road, Marino
☎ 833 1618
🕐 Feb, Mar, Nov, Dec Sat–Sun 12–4; Apr Sat–Sun 12–5; May, Oct daily 10–5; Jun–end Sep daily 10–6; last admission 45 mins before closing
🚆 Clontarf Road
🚌 20A, 20B, 27, 27A, 27B, 27C, 42, 42C
♿ Few
💷 Inexpensive
❓ Visit by guided tour only

HIGHLIGHTS

● Geometrical design
● Corner lions
● Curving wooden doors
● Stucco work
● Marquetry floors

Described as 'a flawless and perfectly cut diamond set into the emerald diadem that is Ireland', the Casino has to be the country's most compact and ingenious 18th-century architectural creation.

Inspiration The Casino is now surrounded by modern suburbia. But when viewed in its original rural setting, this deceptively small building must have resembled a Roman temple in Elysian fields. Its enlightened patron was James Caulfield, fourth Viscount Charlemont (1728–99), whose travels in the Mediterranean inspired him to re-create classical elegance and ingenuity in his homeland. To achieve this, he enticed King George III's architect, Sir William Chambers (1723–96), to design three buildings on his lands. Two survive: the first is his town house, now home to the Hugh Lane gallery (▷ 49), and the second is this delightful house whose name derives from the Italian word *casa*. Curiously, Chambers never came to Ireland to see his masterpiece.

Geometry Its floor plan is a Greek cross encircled by pillars on a raised podium with benign lions at each corner creating a diagonal axis. Columns are water pipes, urns are chimneys. What seems from the outside like a single interior space comprises 16 rooms. The four state rooms on the ground floor are perfect in detail—with curving wooden doors, stucco friezes illustrating musical instruments and agricultural implements, and fine marquetry floors carefully assembled with a variety of rare woods.

The O'Connell monument at Glasnevin (left). A Celtic Cross in the cemetery (right)

Glasnevin

Once the site of a monastery, this leafy suburb has two well-wooded neighbours separated only by a tall stone wall—the National Botanic Gardens and the National Cemetery.

Botanic Gardens Ireland's most extensive and varied collection of plants are carefully tended here. Generously laid out over 19.5ha (47 acres), the gardens were founded in 1795. The curvilinear glass houses, built by Richard Turner, a Dubliner who created a similar structure for Kew Gardens in London, are among the finest surviving examples of 19th-century glass-and-iron construction. Many of the plants housed within originate from southeast Asia; one rarity, the handkerchief tree (so called because the whitish leaves enclosing each flower resemble handkerchiefs), comes from China. An education and visitor facility opened in 2000 gives a good insight into the Botanical Gardens.

Cemetery The adjoining cemetery is reached by a separate entrance just over a mile away. Its graves are a Who's Who of modern Ireland's formative years: Charles Stewart Parnell, Michael Collins and Eamon de Valera. At the foot of Ireland's tallest Round Tower lie the remains of Daniel O'Connell (1775–1847), who founded the cemetery and liberated Irish Catholics from repressive religious legislation. Kavanagh's pub, outside the old entrance, is known locally as the Grave-diggers'; thirsty grave-diggers would pass their shovels through an opening in its wall and a pint of beer was added to restore their spirits.

FARTHER AFIELD

★ **TOP 25**

THE BASICS

Botanic Gardens

🞥 F1

✉ Glasnevin Hill Road

☎ 857 0909 or 837 7596

🕐 Summer: Mon–Sat 9–6, Sun 10–6. Winter: daily 10–4 (glass houses/alpines are restricted)

🚇 Drumcondra

🚌 113, 19, 83

♿ Good except for some glass houses

💲 Free

❓ Guided tours available by prior arrangement

Cemetery

🞥 G1

✉ Finglas Road, Glasnevin

☎ 830 1133

🕐 Mon–Sat 8.30–4.30, Sun 9–4.30

🚇 Drumcondra

🚌 40, 40A, 40B, 40C

♿ Good, except to crypt

💲 Free

❓ Tours Wed, Fri 2.30

HIGHLIGHTS

Botanic Gardens

● Palm house
● Curvilinear glass house
● Last Rose of Summer

Cemetery

● O'Connell's tomb in crypt
● Parnell's grave
● Michael Collins' plot

Kilmainham Gaol

HIGHLIGHTS

● East wing
● 1916 corridor with cells
● Museum display

TIPS

● Ask the guide to shut you into one of the cells and find out what prison life was like.
● If you have limited time miss out the audio-visual presentenation as it is the least exciting part of the tour.

Leading figures in every rebellion against British rule since 1798 are associated with Kilmainham Gaol and, for many Irish people, their imprisonment or death represents freedom through sacrifice.

Prisoners A deserted gaol may seem an unusual place to spend a few hours, but with its stark and severe interiors, Kilmainham has a fascination that is more inspirational than morbid. Opened in 1796, and altered frequently since, the gaol is made up of tall interlinked blocks·in the middle, flanked by exercise and work yards. During the course of its long history, it held both civil and political prisoners, the earliest of whom were participants in the 1798 rebellion. The flow continued throughout the following century and included the 'Young Ireland' rebels of 1848 (Europe's 'Year of

Detail of a cell door in Kilmainham Gaol built in 1792 (left)
The tree-lined pedestrian avenue leading to Kilmainham (below left)
A view of the main compound inside the gaol, which formerly housed generations of Irtish rebels and is now a museum (right)

Revolution'), the Fenian suspects of 1867 and notable parliamentarians in the 1880s.

Conditions Overcrowding created appalling conditions when the Great Famine of 1845–49 drove many to petty crime. Closed in 1910, the gaol was reopened during the 1916 rebellion in Dublin to receive insurgents whose execution in the prison in the May and June of that year turned the tide of public opinion in many parts of Ireland in favour of the armed struggle. During the Civil War of the early 1920s, the gaol again housed anti-government rebels including many women, and four Republican leaders were executed. The doors were closed in 1924, and the abandoned gaol was eventually restored between 1960 and 1984. Cared for by the State, it has an excellent museum display.

THE BASICS

➕ B7
✉ Inchicore Road, Kilmainham
☎ 453 5984
🕐 Apr–end Sep daily 9.30–5; Oct–end Mar Mon–Sat 9.30–5, Sun 10–6; last admission 1 hour before closing
🍴 Tearoom
🚉 Heuston
🚌 68, 69, 79; Luas Heuston
♿ Call in advance for wheelchair assistance
💰 Moderate
❓ Guided tours only–prebook to avoid lines

Irish Museum of Modern Art

Fountain at the Irish Museum of Modern Art (left). Interior gallery (middle). Snowman by Gary Hume (right)

FARTHER AFIELD · TOP 25 · ★

THE BASICS

www.modernart.ie
C7
Royal Hospital, Military Road, Kilmainham
612 9900
Tue–Sat 10–5.30, Sun and public hols 12–5.30
Café
Heuston
26, 51, 51B, 78A, 79, 90, 123; Luas Heuston
Good
Free
Free guided tours of exhibitions Wed and Fri 2.30, Sun 12.15

HIGHLIGHTS

- Covered arcade
- Tympana
- Permanent collections
- Visiting exhibitions

The Royal Hospital at Kilmainham, once a haven for retired soldiers, is now an ultramodern cultural hub where regularly changing exhibitions showcase the latest trends in contemporary art.

Shelter The most important surviving 17th-century building in Ireland, the Royal Hospital at Kilmainham was founded as the Irish equivalent of the Invalides in Paris and the Chelsea pensioners' hospital in London. The architect, surveyor-general Sir William Robinson, laid the structure around an open quadrangle, and created a covered arcade around three sides of the ground floor where residents could stroll outdoors even in poor weather.

Transformation A hospital until 1927, the building was transformed 70 years later into the National Centre for Culture and the Arts, covering music and art. The Irish Museum of Modern Art is Ireland's leading national institution for the collection and presentation of modern and contemporary art. The museum's mission is to foster within society an awareness, understanding and involvement in the visual arts presenting a wide variety of artists' work in an agenda of exhibitions. It possesses its own collections, such as the excellent Madden-Arnholz collection of historic prints (from Dürer onwards) and the New York Portfolio, Gordon Lambert's gift of prints by prominent American artists. Selections are frequently on display on the ground and upper floors, and the museum regularly stages changing exhibitions of modern art from Europe and beyond.

BLESSINGTON STREET GARDEN

A 10-minute walk from O'Connell Street is the former city reservoir, Blessington Street Basin. Here you will find a quiet haven of peace for visitors and local wildlife. Landscaped in the mid-1990s, it remains largely undiscovered and is known as Dublin's secret garden.

➕ F4 ✉ Blessington Street ⏰ Daily during daylight hours 🚌 10 🎫 Free

THE BRAM STOKER DRACULA EXPERIENCE

www.thebramstokerdraculaexperience.com
An experience devoted to Bram Stoker, author of the famous novel *Dracula* (1897). He was born not far from the site of this museum, located in a fitness club close to the Dart station. Not for the faint-hearted, it includes confrontations with Count Dracula in his castle and a visit to the Blood Laboratory at the lunatic asylum.

➕ M3 ✉ Westwood Club, Clontarrf Road ☎ 805 7824 ⏰ Fri 4–10, Sat–Sun 12–10 🚉 Clontarf Road 🚌 20, 20B, 27, 27B, 31, 32 and others ♿ Good 🎫 Expensive

DUBLIN ZOO

www.dublinzoo.ie
More than 700 animals from around the globe live in the 24ha (60 acres) of landscaped grounds of Dublin Zoo, many with plenty of room to roam. Visit Monkey Island, the Arctic Fringes and the World of the Primates, and don't miss the Pet Care Area, Reptile House and Discovery Centre. Experience the African Plains with the Nakuru Safari and check out the newborn babies and feeding times.

➕ B5 ✉ Phoenix Park ☎ 677 1425 ⏰ Mar–end Oct Mon–Sat 9.30–6, Sun 10.30–6; Nov–end Feb Mon–Sat 9.30–dusk, Sun 10.30–dusk 🚌 10, 10A, 25, 26, 66, 66A, 66B, 67, 67A; Luas Heuston 🍴 Restaurant, cafés ♿ Good 🎫 Expensive

GAA MUSEUM

www.gaa.ie
The Gaelic Athletic Association (GAA) is Ireland's largest sporting and cultural organization. Their museum, dedicated to the national games, is housed in the home of Gaelic sport, Croke Park, and is well worth a visit.

Resting on one leg—a stork in the zoo

Meet the elephants at Dublin Zoo

✚ J3 ✉ New Stand, Croke Park, St.
Joseph's Avenue ☎ 855 8176 ⊙ Mon–Sat
9.30–5, Sun 12–5; not open on match days.
Check for stadium tour times 🚌 3, 11, 16

IRISH JEWISH MUSEUM
The synagogue that opened here in
1918 is now a museum dedicated to
the history of Ireland's Jewish community from the mid-19th century to the
present day.
✚ G9 ✉ 4 Walworth Road, off Victoria
Street ☎ 453 1797 ⊙ Oct–end Apr Sun
only 10.30–2.30; May–end Sep Tue, Thu, Sun
11–3.30 🚌 16, 16A, 19, 19A ♿ Few
♨ Free

PEARSE MUSEUM
www.heritageireland.ie
Former school run by Patrick Pearse,
the Dublin-born poet and revolution-
ary executed in 1916 at Kilmainham
Gaol (▷ 94–95).
✚ Off map at F9 ✉ St. Edna's Park, Grange
Road, Rathfarnham ☎ 493 4208 ⊙ Daily
10–1 and Nov–end Jan 2–4; Feb–end Apr,
Sep, Oct 2–5; May–end Aug, 2–5.30 🚌 16
🍴 Tearooms ♿ Ground floor ♨ Free

PHOENIX PARK
A vast expanse of green space, lakes
and woodland in the heart of the city,
this is the largest urban park in
Europe, covering some 696ha (1,720
acres) and encircled by an 13km (8-
mile) wall. Within its confines are
Dublin Zoo (▷ 97), the American
Ambassador's home and the Irish
President's residence, Áras an
Uachtaráin. The visitor area is on the
site of the old Papal Nunciature.
✚ A5 🚌 25, 25A, 26, 51; Luas Heuston
(Parkgate Street entrance) ♨ Visitor centre
inexpensive; park free

WAR MEMORIAL GARDENS
These wonderful gardens are dedicated to the 49,400 Irish soldiers who
died in World War I. Especially moving
are the thousands of names etched in
the granite book rooms and the beautiful sunken rose gardens. Rowers can
sometimes be seen gliding along the
River Liffey. Well off the tourist beat.
✚ A7 ✉ Islandbridge ☎ 677 0236
⊙ Mon–Fri 8–dusk, Sat–Sun 10–dusk
🚌 25, 25A, 51, 66, 66A, 69 ♨ Free

Golden harp at the Memorial Gardens (above). Mural at the Sentana Centre (right)

Dublin from the DART

BLIN AREA RAPID TRANSIT

VIEWS FROM THE DART

- Dalkey Island off Killiney
- Sailboats off Dun Laoghaire
- Blackrock's public park and private gardens
- Wetlands bird sanctuary at Booterstown
- Custom House between Tara Street and Connolly Station
- Urban jungle of Kilbarrack, backdrop for novels *The Commitments*, *The Snapper* and *The Van*, Roddy Doyle's prize-winning trilogy

BRAY

This attractive seaside town, towards the southern end of the DART line, has become a playground for the young at heart who come for the amusements, bumper cars and fortune-tellers operating on the promenade most of the year round. There are fine walks and splendid views around nearby Bray Head.

DUN LAOGHAIRE

Invigorating walks along the piers at Dun Laoghaire, a Victorian seaside resort once known as Kingstown, are something of a Dublin institution. The scenery is stunning, and you can see the fer-ries plying to and fro across the Irish Sea. The East Pier has a bandstand, folk dancers, rollerbladers and a busy stream of pedestrians. The longer West Pier on the other side attracts fishing enthusiasts.

HOWTH

This promontory to the north of Dublin is a tradi-tional fishing village and trendy suburb in one. A popular sailing hub, the Howth marina is always packed with yachts from Ireland and abroad. Howth DART station is near the harbour and close to all the waterside activity, bars and restaurants. Howth is idyllic in sunny weather, and is very busy over the Easter holiday when the place buzzes dur-ing one of Ireland's major jazz festivals.

Fishing boats in the harbour at Howth

Bray Head promenade (above right)
Kilruddery House, Bray (right)

DART DUBLIN AREA RAPID TRANSIT

KILLINEY

National and international celebrities such as Bono, Damon Hill, Neil Jordan and Eddie Irvine have settled in the resort known affectionately as Dublin's Riviera. Take a walk along the Vico Road for what is arguably the most breathtaking view in Dublin. Look out to Dalkey Island, a craggy piece of land captured by the Vikings and later the site of Christian communities. Fishermen in nearby Coliemore Harbour run boat trips in summer to view the resident goats, the ruined oratory and the Martello Tower.

SANDYCOVE

Just south of Dun Laoghaire and accessible by the DART is the popular commuter village of Sandycove, famous for its seaside promenade, which runs all the way to Dun Laoghaire. It is named after a small sandy cover near the rocky point on which a Martello tower was built during the Napoleonic Wars. James Joyce chose the Martello Tower along the waterfront as the setting for the first chapter of *Ulysses* and the museum inside (☎ 280 9265 for opening times) displays Joycean memorabilia, including letters, photographs and items such as his guitar. A bracing swim in the sea here may introduce you to other die-hards who take the plunge all year around.

DALKEY

Only a few stops south on the DART and you'll find yourself in the attractive former fishing village of Dalkey, well known for its literary associations. George Bernard Shaw lived in the village and James Joyce set chapter two of *Ulyssess* here. The Heritage Centre is accessed through Goat Castle in Castle Street and from the battlements you get a splendid view of the sea and mountains. Good pubs and restaurants enhance your visit.

FARTHER AFIELD

★

DUBLIN FROM THE DART

View from Dalkey Hill across Killiney Bay towards the distant Wicklow Hills

St. Kevin's Church, Glendalough (▷ 102)

Excursions

THE BASICS

THE BASICS

Distance: 64km (40 miles)
Journey Time: 1 hour
30 mins
✉ Brú Na Bóinne Visitor
Centre, Donore, Co Meath
☎ 041 988 0300
🕐 Daily 9.30–5.30 (9–7 in
high season). Tours last 1
hour 15 mins; last tour 1
hour 45 mins before closing
🚌 Bus Éireann 100 to
Drogheda, then 163 to
Donore village (10-min
walk). Also bus tours

BRÚ NA BÓINNE

**A desiganted UNESCO World Heritage
Site, Brú Na Bóinne is one of the most
important prehistoric monuments in
Europe.**

'The Palace of the Boyne' is the name given to a
large group of neolithic remains in the central
Boyne Valley 11km (7 miles) west of Drogheda.
The huge, white-fronted passage tomb of
Newgrange is the best known, but the nearby
mounds of Knowth and Dowth were probably of
equal importance historically. These great tombs
are more than 5,000 years old. You can only visit
the main site with a tour from the visitor centre.

THE BASICS

Distance: 48km (30 miles)
Journey Time: 1 hour
15 mins
☎ 404 45325
🕐 Visitor centre mid-Mar
to mid-Oct 9.30–6, 9–5 rest
of year
🚌 Glendalough bus from
Bray and Dublin. Can be
reached on coach tours
from Dublin. The most
direct route if driving is the
N11 (M11) south

GLENDALOUGH

**Glendalough ('valley of two lakes') was
one of Ireland's most venerated monasteries. Its setting makes it one of eastern
Ireland's premier attractions.**

Situated at the end of a long valley stretching
deep into the Wicklow hills, it grew up around the
tomb of its founder, St. Kevin. He was abbot of
Glendalough until his death in AD618 and the
monastery became famous throughout Europe as
a seat of learning. The core of the old monastery
consists of a roofless cathedral (c900), a well-pre-
served Round Tower and St. Kevin's Church,
roofed with stone. Overlooking the Upper Lake,
about a mile away, is another enchanting church
called Reefert. There are good walks in the sur-
rounding woods. The visitor centre also acts as an
information outlet for the Wicklow Mountains
National Park. Being such an important attraction it
can get very busy in high summer.

MALAHIDE CASTLE

Malahide Castle stands in a wooded area, north of Dublin.

Apart from an interlude during the rule of Oliver Cromwell, the castle stayed in the hands of the Talbot family from c1200 until 1976. The core of the castle is a medieval tower and in the adjoining banqueting hall the walls are hung with portraits. Most furnishings are Georgian. A separate building houses the beautifully detailed rolling stock of the Fry Model Railway. Outside are opportunities for walking and the Talbot Botanic Gardens (🕐 May to end Sep).

THE BASICS

Distance: 13km (8 miles)
Journey Time: 45 mins
☎ 846 2184
🕐 Mon–Sat 10–5; also Apr–end Sep Sun 9–6; Oct–end Mar Sun 11–5
🚌 42
🚆 From Connolly Station to Malahide, then a 10-min walk

POWERSCOURT

Beautifully set in the heart of the wild Wicklow Mountains, yet only a hour from Dublin, this house is renowned for its magnificent gardens.

Careful restoration has converted the 18th-century Palladian mansion into an excellent gallery of shops with a terrace restaurant. It is in a dramatic setting, with the cone-shaped Sugar Loaf mountain in the distance. To the south, the house looks out over magnificently proportioned stepped terraces, with ornamental sculpture and a statue throwing a jet of water high in the air. Gardens stretch to either side; the one to the east is Japanese, the other walled with wrought-iron Bavarian gates. (The story goes that when the terraces' designer, Daniel Robertson, went to inspect the work every morning, he was pushed around in a wheelbarrow, swigging sherry.) You can walk to the waterfall 5km (3 miles) away, but it is easier to get there by car.

THE BASICS

Distance: 19km (12 miles)
Journey Time: 1 hour
☎ 204 6000
🕐 9.30–5.30 (gardens close at dusk)
🚌 44
🚆 DART to Bray, then 185 feeder bus to Enniskerry
❓ Waterfall inadvisable on foot

FARTHER AFIELD
EXCURSIONS

Shopping

BLACKROCK MARKET
www.blackrockmarket.ie
Established in 1996, bargain hunters flock to Blackrock, 8km (5 miles) south of Dublin, for the market held every Saturday 11–5.30 and Sunday 12–5.30. Also holiday Mondays 11–5.30. Stalls sell clothes, bric-à-brac, fine art, crafts and antiques. There are usually around 50 traders plus refreshment stands.
➕ Off map ✉ Blackrock 🚆 Blackrock 🚌 7, 7A, 8, 17

BLANCHARDSTOWN CENTRE
www.blanchardstowncentre.ie
A massive mall, one of Ireland's biggest, is about a 20-minute drive northwest from town and has supermarkets, department stores, cinemas and, more importantly, the best selection of price-wise and fashionable local and international retail names under one roof in the Dublin area.
➕ Off map
✉ Blanchardstown
🚆 Suburban line Connolly to Blanchardstown 🚌 38, 38A, 39, 39X, 70, 70X, 236

OUT OF TOWN
There is an excellent modern shopping mall at The Square in Tallaght, just south of Dublin. It is the largest in Ireland with nearly 150 shops under a huge dome of natural light. This creates perfect conditions for trees and shrubs to thrive, giving the sense of being outdoors but without the rain. Open daily, the shopping mall has a large UCI cinema, fast-food restaurants, a free crèche, a bowling alley, plenty of pubs nearby and parking for some 3,000 cars.

DOUGLAS FOOD COMPANY
Epicurean haven for those in a hurry, with the best caviar, foie gras, pastries, wines and French cheese. Also a take out with homemade soups, sandwiches and yummy desserts. Why not try the wonderful Bailey's loaf, a perfect accompaniment to coffee.
➕ Off map ✉ 53 Main Street, Donnybrook 🕿 269 4066 🚌 10, 46a

LIFFEY VALLEY SHOPPING CENTRE
www.liffeyvalley.ie
A 20-minute drive southwest of the city with more than 90 retail outlets. The food-court has 12 restaurants and cafés including Eddie Rockets Diner and Harry Ramsden's. A retail park boasts many top names.
➕ Off map ✉ Fonthill Road, Clondalkin 🚌 78A

Entertainment and Nightlife

BLANCHARDSTOWN UCI
A nine-screen multiplex outside the city with a comprehensive choice. Films tend to run longer here than at the more central cinemas.
➕ Off map
✉ Blanchardstown Shopping Centre 🕿 812 8383
🚆 Suburban line Connolly to Blanchardstown 🚌 38, 38A, 39, 39X, 70, 70X, 236

CIVIC THEATRE
www.civictheatre.ie
A community arts venue in the southwest suburbs providing mainstream drama and classical music concerts, traditional and contemporary music. Art gallery, café and bar.
➕ Off map ✉ Blessington Road, off Belguard Square East, Tallght 🕿 707 4100 🚌 49A, 50Xm 54A, 77A, 77X

GAELIC GAMES
www.gaa.ie; www.crokepark.ie
Gaelic football and hurling are fast, physical

games, and the All-Ireland finals are played before sell-out crowds in early and late September. Immensely popular.

🚉 J3 ⊠ Croke Park Stadium, St. Joseph's Avenue ☎ 819 2300 🚌 3, 11, 16, 51A

THE HELIX
www.thehelix.ie
Opened in 2002, this complex at the City Univeristy has three auditoria—the 1,260-capacity Mahony Hall, the 450-seat Theatre and the 150-seat Space—serving up a flexible mix of classical concerts, drama and rock and pop music.

🚉 Off map ⊠ Dublin City University, Collins Avenue, Glasnevin ☎ 700 7000 🚌 13, 18, 83

HORSE RACING
Leopardstown Race Course is one of Ireland's busiest. Open all year, it hosts the Hennessy Gold Cup and a traditional post-Christmas festival, among other events.

🚉 Off map ⊠ Shillorgan Road, Foxrock ☎ 289 0500 🚌 86, 118

JOHNNIE FOX'S
www.jfp.ie
People come from near and far for the turf fires, live traditional music, céilí dancing and delicious seafood. If you want to eat, be sure to reserve ahead.

🚉 Off map ⊠ Glencullen, County Dublin ☎ 295 5647 🚌 44B

ORMONDE
www.ormondecinemas.com
The only movie theatre worth visting on Dublin's south side. Five screens show a mixture of new releases and kids' movies.

🚉 Off map ⊠ Lower Kilmacud Road, Stillorgan ☎ 707 4100 🚌 46A

ROLLERBLADING
The smooth, flat, picturesque walk along Sandymount Strand is popular with local in-line skaters who whoosh along the waterfront day and night. A stunning location in spring and summer.

🚉 Off map ⊠ Sandymount Strand, Sandymount 🚌 2, 3

RUGBY
Ireland's fans are always enthusiastic when it comes to their national team. Details of fixtures for local clubs, like Bective

GOLF

The growth of championship golf courses in Dublin is staggering—the 2006 Ryder Cup was held at the K Club near Dublin. Many clubs welcome nonmembers, and fees are reasonable. The most famous are Portmarnock and Royal Dublin; also try Castle, Grange, Woodbrook Malahide, Miltown, Hermitage and Island, or try one of the city's pitch-and-putt courses. The Irish Open Golf Championships are staged in July.

Rangers, Wesley and Blackrock are published in the local press. With Lansdowne Road closed for renovation until at least 2008, all international and top games will be played at Croke Park (▷ 104). You could watch a game in one of the many pubs showing the match on screen.

🚉 M9 ⊠ Lansdowne Road Stadium, Ballsbridge ☎ 668 4601 🚇 Lansdowne Road 🚌 5, 7, 7A, 45

SOCCER
Since the World Cup in 1990, the Irish have become soccer fanatics, and Dublin usually stands still when the national team plays. The season runs from March to November, and you can buy tickets for matches at Tolka Park Stadium (shared home to Shamrock Rovers and Shelbourne Rovers), at the gate.

🚉 J2 ⊠ Tolka Park Stadium, Richmond Road ☎ 837 5536 🚌 11, 11A, 13A, 41, 41A, 41B,

STER CENTURY
www.stercentury.ie
Ireland's biggest and newest multiplex cinema has 14 screens including the Big Fella, Europe's largest. Seats look and feel like sports cars, and sound and picture quality are state-of-the-art, as are the eating facilities.

🚉 Off map ⊠ Liffey Valley Centre, Fonthill Road, Clondalkin ☎ 605 5700 🚌 78A

FARTHER AFIELD

ENTERTAINMENT AND NIGHTLIFE

Restaurants

PRICES

Prices are approximate, based on a 3-course meal for one person.

€€€	over €40
€€	€20–€40
€	under €20

BAHAY KUBO (€€)

For unique Filipino cuisine such as *Sinigang Na Manok*—hot and sour chicken soup with chili, lemon grass and lime leaves. The dishes have influences from Taiwan to Thailand.
➕ Off map ✉ 14 Bath Avenue, Sandymount ☎ 660 5572 🚆 Sandymount
🚌 2, 3, 18

BELLA CUBA (€€)

www.bella-cuba.com
Tasty Cuban dishes served with a smile in a tropical atmosphere accompanied by salsa music.
➕ Off map ✉ 11 Ballsbridge Terrace ☎ 660 5539 🕐 Lunch Mon–Fri, dinner daily 🚆 Lansdowne Road
🚌 Cross-city buses

BRASSERIE NA MARA (€€€)

A sophisticated, deceptively grand restaurant, frequented by well-heeled locals and the expense account set. The emphasis is on fresh, local seafood.
➕ Off map ✉ The Harbour, Dun Laoghaire ☎ 280 6767 🕐 Lunch Mon–Fri, dinner Mon–Sat 🚆 Dun Laoghaire
🚌 7, 8

CAVISTONS (€€)

www.cavistons.com
Immensely popular restaurant that arose from the success of the neighbouring shop. Modern fresh food with a Mediterranean slant.
➕ Off map ✉ 59 Glasthule Road, Sandycove ☎ 280 9245 🕐 Lunch Tue–Sat 🚆 Sandycove and Glasthule
🚌 59

DOCKERS (€)

Basic quayside pub frequented by old-style Dubliners as well as actors, film folk and musicians. Made fashionable by the likes of U2 and Jim Sheridan, this is one of the city's best places for sausage sandwiches and pints of Guinness.
➕ L6 ✉ 5 Sir John Rogerson's Quay ☎ 677 1692 🕐 Food served at lunch

AVOCA CAFÉS

The Avoca Handweavers were founded in 1723 and in recent years their award-winning cafés have been talked about as much as their famous shops. You can find branches in the village of Avoca, the home of the original mill, at Kilmacanoge near Bray, at Powerscourt House (▷ 103) and in the middle of Dublin in Suffolk Street. Homemade is the key word and the desserts are especially noteworthy plus the great scones, biscuits and cakes.

only 🚆 Grand Canal Dock
🚌 1, 3,

GUINEA PIG (THE FISH RESTAURANT) (€€€)

www.guineapig.dalkey.info
Attractive, family-run restaurant, with an extensive, though not exclusively, seafood-based menu. In business since 1957.
➕ Off map ✉ 17 Railway Road, Dalkey ☎ 285 9055 🕐 Dinner only 🚆 Dalkey
🚌 59, 59A

HARBOURMASTER BAR AND RESTAURANT (€€–€€€)

www.harbourmaster.ie
Located in the old Dock Offices in the heart of the growing financial district and with a waterside setting, the Greenhouse Restaurant serves an interesting and varied international menu.
➕ J6 ✉ Custom House Dock ☎ 670 1688 🕐 Greenhouse restaurant lunch only Mon–Fri; bar and brasserie daily 🚆 Connolly

KING SITRIC (€€€)

www.kingsitric.ie
The fish are landed a few yards from Dublin's most regal seafood restaurant, named after the 11th-centry Norse king of Dublin. Popular with Dublin high society. Wonderful menu and wine cellar.
➕ Off map ✉ East Pier, Howth ☎ 832 5235 🕐 Lunch Mon–Fri, dinner Mon–Sat 🚆 Howth 🚌 31

From boutique hotels to elegant Georgian townhouses, there are some great choices when deciding where to stay in Dublin but it's expensive. North of the river bed-and-breakfast is a less expensive option.

Introduction

Dublin is an expensive place for a visit but, depending on where you choose to stay, you can still manage to find some bargain accommodations. North of the River Liffey is less expensive than south or you could opt to stay in the quieter suburbs getting into the city by bus, DART or Luas tram.

Accommodation Options

Exclusive hotels in the heart of the city and in particular around St. Stephen's Green and Merrion Square offer high standards and prices to match. For good quality but better value try the townhouses or stay in the suburbs. Hostels offer the cheapest budget options in the city and although some have shared facilites they are increasingly offering more private rooms. Room rates for all levels fluctuate during the year, peaking from June to September. Be sure to ask about special offers when making your reservation. Some hotels, particularly chains, have special midweek or weekend rates at certain times of the year. Rates usually include full Irish breakfast.

Reservation Advice

It is strongly advisable to reserve rooms in advance in Dublin as it is an extremely popular destination and although accommodation levels have risen since the mid-1990s, the demand is ever increasing. During special events such as the rugby internationals the city can become full to bursting, causing the restaurants, bars and pubs to become very overcrowded. Reservations for hotels can be made online through Fáilte Ireland Tourist Board at www.ireland.travel.ie. If you have not booked in advance Dublin Tourism in Suffolk Street offers an on-the-spot booking service for a small fee.

Self-Catering

Most of the accommodations are located outside the city, in the suburbs or by the coast. There are, however, more central options available. Check out www.visitdublin.com.

There is plenty of choice when staying in Dublin from Georgian townhouses to modern hotels

Budget Hotels

PRICES

Expect to pay under €100 for a double room in a budget hotel

AVALON HOUSE
www.avalon-house.ie
This purpose-built hostel offers 65 single or double rooms and six dormitory rooms, in neat, fresh surroundings. Café and use of Internet.
➕ G8 ✉ 55 Aungier Street ☎ 475 000 🚌 Cross-city buses

BARNACLES TEMPLE BAR HOUSE
www.barnacles.ie
Hostel with communal TV room, self-catering facilities and breakfast room. Dormitory-style rooms, all with shower. Great for the buzz of Temple Bar.
➕ G7 ✉ 19 Temple Lane South ☎ 671 6277 🚇 Tara Street 🚌 Cross-city buses

BEWLEY'S NEWLANDS CROSS
www.bewleyshotels.com
Good amenities and spacious 258 bedrooms, furnished to a high standard. Slightly outside the city so best if you have a car.
➕ Off map ✉ Newland's Cross, Naas Road ☎ 871 1000 🚌 51

HARDING HOTEL
www.hardinghotel.ie
A superior find in the budget bracket, Hardings looks the part with clever interior design and is

packed with atmosphere thanks to a lively hotel bar. 53 rooms.
➕ G7 ✉ Copper Alley, Fishamble Street ☎ 679 6500 🚌 Cross-city buses

KINLAY HOUSE
www.kinlayhouse.ie
A good hostel with 39 rooms to suit different budgets—from dormitory-style to en-suite twins. Continental breakfast included. Can be noisy at night.
➕ G7 ✉ 2–12 Lord Edward Street ☎ 679 6644 🚌 Cross-city buses

MARIAN GUEST HOUSE
www.marianguesthouse.ie
In elegant Georgian Dublin, 5 to 10 minutes' walk from the city hub and principal attractions. Family run, offering a warm welcome and six tastefully decorated rooms with tea- and coffee making facilities.
➕ H4 ✉ 21 Gardiner Street Upper ☎ 874 4129 🚇 Connolly 🚌 41A

BUDGET STAY

Budget accommodation in Dublin comes in three different formats:
● Hotels—New, functional and clean.
● Hostels—Good selection of low-cost hostels often with cafés and Internet.
● Guesthouses—Reputable B&Bs listed with the tourist office.

ORMOND QUAY HOTEL
www.ormondquayhotel.ie
Overlooking the River Liffey and offering a friendly and welcoming atmosphere. 60 rooms.
➕ G6 ✉ 7–11 Ormond Quay Upper ☎ 872 1811; fax 872 1362 🚇 Tara Street 🚌 Cross-city buses

OLIVER ST. JOHN GOGARTY
www.gogarty.ie
Gogarty's offer budget rooms right in the heart of Temple Bar. Be prepared for a lively stay with the bar and restaurant always packed and plenty of traditional music in the upstairs bar.
➕ H7 ✉ 18–21 Anglesea Street ☎ 671 1822 🚇 Connolly 🚌 Cross-city buses

O'SHEAS
www.osheas hotel.com
Warm and friendly hotel close to the shopping districts and sights, with 34 attractive rooms, bar, lounge and restaurant.
➕ H5 ✉ 19 Talbot Street ☎ 836 5670 🚇 Connolly 🚌 Cross-city buses

TRINITY COLLEGE
If you are planning a long stay in the summer, it is possible to rent student rooms in Trinity College at reasonable rates. Some have their own bathrooms and kitchens.
➕ H7 ✉ College Green ☎ 608 1177; fax 671 1267 🚇 Pearse Tara Street 🚌 Cross-city buses

Mid-Range Hotels

PRICES

Expect to pay between €100 and €200 for a double room in a mid-range hotel

ABBERLEY COURT
www.abberley.ie
Next to an excellent complex of shops, restaurants and a cinema, this 40-room smart hotel includes two bars, a carvery and a Chinese restaurant.
➕ Off map ✉ Belgard Road, Tallaght ☎ 459 6000 🚌 49, 65, 65B, 77

ARIEL HOUSE
www.ariel-house.net
A gracious Victorian house in the suburb of Ballsbridge. Good standard in all 37 rooms; tasty breakfasts—with vegetarian options—and aromatherapy and reflexology treatments. You are well treated by the friendly staff. Secure parking.
➕ L9 ✉ 50–54 Landsdowne Road, Ballsbridge ☎ 668 5512 🚊 Lansdowne Road 🚌 7, 45

ASTON HOTEL
www.aston-hotel.com
Tranquil hotel situated in the middle of Temple Bar that manages to convey a feeling of calm while all outside is hectic. Popular with groups. This hotel is at the top end of price range. 27 rooms.
➕ H6 ✉ 7–9 Aston Quay ☎ 677 9300 🚌 Cross-city buses

BLAKES TOWNHOUSE
www.halspinsprivatehotels.com
Refurbished to a high standard. Some of the 13 rooms have balconies overlooking the gardens.
➕ Off map ✉ 50 Merrion Road, Ballsbridge ☎ 668 8324 🚌 Sandymount 🚌 7, 45

CASSIDY'S HOTEL
www.cassidyshotel.com
Family-run, 88-room hotel in a Georgian terrace at the top end of O'Connell Street. Grooms Bar and Restaurant 6 are an added bonus. Parking places are limited.
➕ H5 ✉ Cavendish Row, O'Connell Street Upper ☎ 888 0555 🚌 Cross-city buses

DEER PARK HOTEL & GOLF COURSES
www.deerpark-hotel.ie
Only 14km (8.5 miles)

OTHER OPTIONS

Staying in Dublin can be an expensive business. You might consider staying a bit farther out where the tariffs are cheaper but it will mean a short bus ride or taking a taxi into the city. If you have a car you could stay even further out in the quieter, more relaxing suburbs or on the coast at Portmarnock. It is worth trying some of the smaller Georgian townhouses that have been converted into small hotels or guesthouses, which are often better value.

from the heart of the city and situated on a quiet hillside overlooking the sea, the Deer Park features Ireland's largest golf complex with five courses including a 6,104m (6,678 yard), par 72, 18-hole course.
➕ Off map ✉ Howth ☎ 832 2624

GRAFTON CAPITAL
www.capital-hotels.com
In the heart of Dublin's shopping and cultural area, with many restaurants, cafés and attractions just around the corner. Traditional Georgian townhouse with friendly and helpful staff, and 75 modern rooms.
➕ G7 ✉ Stephen's Street Lower ☎ 648 1100 🚊 Pearse 🚌 Cross-city buses

GRAND CANAL HOTEL
www.grandcanalhotel.com
Part of the Cara chain and opened in 2004 as part of the new canal complex, this purpose-built hotel has 142 rooms.
➕ L8 ✉ 13–27 Grand Canal Street ☎ 646 1000 🚊 Grand Canal Dock 🚌 5, 7, 7A, 45

HARRINGTON HALL
www.harringtonhall.com
A beautifully restored Georgian guesthouse with genteel public areas and 28 generously proportioned guest rooms. An elegant address in the city hub.

➕ G9 ✉ 70 Harcourt Street
☎ 475 3497 🚌 Cross-city
buses

JURYS INN CHRISTCHURCH
www.bookajurysinn.com
Rates are calculated on a
per room basis (up to
three adults, or two adults
with two children). Lovely
bar and restaurant plus a
parking area. 182 rooms.
➕ F7 ✉ Christchurch Place
☎ 454 0000 🚌 Cross-city
buses

LONGFIELDS
www.longfields.ie
Longfields has a warm,
hospitable feel. Staff are
focused on guest care in
an informal, yet profes-
sional, manner. The 26
rooms vary in size but are
very comfortable. The
Longchamp @ No. 10
restaurant (▷ 87) serves
first-class modern Irish
cuisine.
➕ J8 ✉ 10 Fitzwilliam Street
Lower ☎ 676 1367
🚇 Pearse 🚌 Cross-city buses

THE MERCER HOTEL
www.mercerhotel.ie
A modern hotel with 41
en-suite rooms that is
close to Grafton Street
and St. Stephen's Green.
Attractive, well-equipped
bedrooms plus cocktail
lounge and restaurant.
➕ G8 ✉ Mercer Street
Lower ☎ 478 2179
🚇 Pearse 🚌 Cross-city buses

MESPIL
www.leehotels.com
Efficient, spacious and
modern; 255 rooms,
some overlooking the
Grand Canal.
➕ J9 ✉ Mespil Road
☎ 488 4600 🚇 Grand Canal
Dock 🚌 10, 11

MOLESWORTH COURT
www.molesworthcourt.ie
These pleasantly decorat-
ed one- and two-bed-
room apartments (12 in
all) can be rented for one
night or more. Quiet, and
near Grafton Street.
➕ H8 ✉ Schoolhouse Lane,
off Molesworth Street ☎ 676
4799 🚇 Pearse 🚌 Cross-
city buses

THE MORGAN
www.themorgan.com
This gem of a hotel has
Egyptian cotton sheets
spacious bathrooms, and
excellent in-room facilities

GOLF HOTELS
Ireland's reputation as a
world-class golfing destination is now undisputed and
there are some excellent
hotels with great courses just
outside the city. Try the
Portmarnock Hotel and Golf
Links renowned for comfort,
good food and world-class
golf. The hotel's 18-hole
course was designed by
Bernard Langer. Near the
airport.
➕ Off map ✉ Strand Road
Portmarnock ☎ 846 0611;
www.portmarnock.com
For another golf hotel option
see opposite page for the
Deer Park Hotel.

including ISDN lines,
VCRs and compact disc
players. 61 rooms.
➕ H6 ✉ 10 Fleet Street,
Temple Bar ☎ 643 7000
🚇 Tara Street 🚌 Cross-city
buses

PEMBROKE TOWN-HOUSE
www.pembroketownhouse.ie
The excellent service in
this Georgian-style
house has won it a loyal
following. Executive
boardroom and access
to local health club. 45
rooms.
➕ L9 ✉ 90 Pembroke
Road ☎ 660 0277
🚇 Lansdowne Road 🚌 5,
7, 7A, 10

STAUNTON'S ON THE GREEN
www.stauntononthegreen.ie
Large Georgian guest-
house with garden and
30 well-equipped
rooms. Perfectly placed
close to museums,
shops and several com-
mercial art galleries.
➕ H8 ✉ 83 St. Stephen's
Green ☎ 478 2300/478
2133 🚇 Pearse 🚌 Cross-
city buses

TEMPLE BAR
www.templebarhotel.com
In the heart of Temple
Bar and close to all the
city sights and entertain-
ments. With 129 rooms,
the hotel is well
equipped and has the
benefit of the on-the-
spot Buskers bar.
➕ H6 ✉ Fleet Street
☎ 677 3333 🚇 Tara Street
🚌 Cross-city buses

Luxury Hotels

WHERE TO STAY LUXURY HOTELS

PRICES

Expect to pay over €200 for a double room in a luxury hotel

BERKELEY COURT
www.jurys-dublin-hotels.com
Superlative comfort and tranquillity with chintz sofas, thick carpets and blissful quiet. 188 rooms.
🚇 L9 ✉ Lansdowne Road
☎ 660 1711 🚋 Lansdowne Road 🚌 5, 7

CLARENCE
www.theclarence.ie
Chic, modern interior with soft suede uphol-stery and stunning floral arrangements. The 50 rooms are small, apart from the fine duplex penthouse. This is a very individual hotel, where contemporary design is tastefully incorporated into the original features of the 1850 building. The Tea Room restaurant at the Clarence is a real treat (▷ 44).
🚇 G7 ✉ 6–8 Wellington Quay ☎ 407 0800
🚋 Tara Street
🚌 Cross-city buses

FITZWILLIAM
www.fitzwilliamhotel.com
A great combination of contemporary style and Irish warmth in a central location. Some of the 130 bedrooms overlook an internal rooftop garden.
🚇 H8 ✉ St. Stephen's Green
☎ 478 7000 🚋 Pearse
🚌 Cross-city buses

GRESHAM
www.gresham-hotels.com
Ultimate luxury and atten-tive service. The 288, huge, elegant bedrooms combine traditional style with modern comfort. Several bars and lounges, the Aberdeen restaurant and a fitness suite.
🚇 H5 ✉ O'Connell Street Upper ☎ 874 6881
🚋 Connolly 🚌 Cross-city buses

HERBERT PARK
www.herbertparkhotel.ie
Modern, bright, airy hotel in Dublin's exclusive resi-dential area. Quiet com-fort with 153 rooms over-looking the peaceful Herbert Park.
🚇 Off map ✉ Herbert Park, Ballsbridge ☎ 667 2200
🚋 Lansdowne Road 🚌 7, 45

MERRION
www.merrionhotel.com
This impressive hotel, originally four Georgian houses, has 140 luxurious bedrooms. Gym, pool and spa. Business facilities.

THE SHELBOURNE
At the time of writing this illustrious hotel was undergo-ing an extensive restoration project. But no guide book to Dublin would be complete without a reference to the Shelbourne on St. Stephen's Green. Hosting the royal and famous since its opening in the 18th century, if you can't afford to stay here why not drop in for afternoon tea.

🚇 J8 ✉ Merrion Street Upper ☎ 603 0600
🚋 Pearse 🚌 Cross-city buses

THE MORRISON
www.morrisonhotel.ie
Modern designer heaven, the Morrison is east-meets-west cosmopolitan. 138 rooms plus lobby bars and restaurants. New in 2006 is the 'well-being' spa complete with Turkish baths, perfect after all that shopping.
🚇 G6 ✉ Ormond Quay Lower ☎ 8874200 🚌 Cross-city buses

SCHOOLHOUSE HOTEL
www.schoolhousehotel.com
Former Victorian school-house, by the Grand Canal, converted into a first-class hotel. It had a complete refurbish-ment in 2006. 31 rooms.
🚇 L9 ✉ 2–8 Northumberland Road
☎ 667 5014 🚋 Grand Canal Dock 🚌 5, 7, 7A, 45

STEPHEN'S HALL
www.stephens-hall.com
Tastefully furnished and all 34 rooms have state-of-the-art office facilities.
🚇 H9 ✉ 14–17 Leeson Street Lower ☎ 638 1111; fax 638 1122 🚌 Cross-city buses

WESTBURY
www.jurys-dublin-hotels.com
Stylish hotel with 205 rooms—popular with celebrities and shoppers.
🚇 H7 ✉ Grafton Street
☎ 679 1122 🚋 Pearse
🚌 Cross-city buses

Dublin is compact and easy to get around on foot. However, buses are numerous and frequent and the DART is great to use for a trip outside the city. Dublin is a fairly safe city but keep alert against petty crime.

Need to Know

Planning Ahead

When to Go

Most visitors come between March and October, when the weather is at its best and there is a wider choice of activities. The best lodging deals are available from November to February, but some attractions are closed. Dublin is temperate year-round but rain is frequent.

TIME

Ireland is five hours ahead of New York, eight hours ahead of Los Angeles and the same as London.

AVERAGE DAILY MAXIMUM TEMPERATURES

JAN	FEB	MAR	APR	MAY	JUN	JUL	AUG	SEP	OCT	NOV	DEC
46°F	46°F	50°F	55°F	59°F	64°F	68°F	66°F	63°F	57°F	50°F	46°F
8°C	8°C	10°C	13°C	15°C	18°C	20°C	19°C	17°C	14°C	10°C	8°C

Spring (March to May) is mild with mostly clear skies and a mix of sunshine and showers. April and May are the driest months.

Summer (June to August) is bright and warm but notoriously unpredictable. July is particularly showery. Heat-waves are rare.

Autumn (September to November) often has very heavy rain and is mostly overcast, although still quite mild. Even October can be summery.

Winter (December to February) is not usually severe and tends to be wet rather than snowy. Temperatures rarely fall below freezing.

WHAT'S ON

February/March *Dublin Film Festival.*

March *St. Patrick's Day Festival* (15–18 Mar). *St. Patrick's Day* (17 Mar).

April *Dublin Opera Spring Season.*

April–May *Heineken Green Energy Festival.*

International Dance festival; for the best in contemporary dance from abstract to ballet.

June *Music Festival in Great Irish Houses;* usually includes a number within easy reach of Dublin.

Bloomsday (12–16 Jun): the hero of James Joyce's novel *Ulysses* is celebrated in word, walks and liquid refreshment.

July *International Summer School* at University College Dublin.

Guinness Blues Festival.

August *Kerrygold Dublin Horse Show* in the Royal Dublin Society grounds.

September *All Ireland Hurling and Gaelic Football Finals.*

Dublin Jazz Week.

September/October *Dublin Theatre Festival;* Europe's oldest specialist theatre event.

Dublin City Marathon.

December *Dublin Antiques & Fine Arts Fair.*

National Crafts Fair.

Christmas Carols in St. Patrick's Cathedral (selected Sundays and special dates).

Dublin Opera Winter Season.

Listings

The daily newspapers, both morning and evening, provide good coverage of what's on in Dublin. Pick up a copy of *In Dublin,* printed every two weeks, and look for *The Event Guide,* free from clubs, cafés and restaurants around the capital. Both list events.

Useful Websites

www.irish-architecture.com
Archéire (architecture eireann) is a diverse selection of architecturally interesting sites with the emphasis ranging from history and preservation to current architectural developments.

www.templebar.ie
The official site of Temple Bar Properties, a company established in 1991 to revitalize the area as a cultural quarter. The site offers an insight into Temple Bar today, what the area has to offer, events and future developments.

www.ireland.com
An influential website of one of Ireland's daily newspapers, the *Irish Times*. You can check out what's on in Dublin and reserve accommodations online.

www.heritageireland.ie
This website contains useful in-depth information about six National Cultural Institutions, historical sites, gardens and inland waterways managed by Dúchas, the Heritage Service.

www.eventguide.ie
A comprehensive guide that dispenses details about forthcoming events at venues across Dublin, from theatre and cinema to live music and comedy.

www.ireland.travel.ie
The main Irish Tourist Board site carries a wealth of information on everything you need to know about the whole of Ireland. There are sections on history, culture, events, activities, accommodations and gastronomy, as well as plenty of practical tips.

www.visitdublin.com
The local tourist board site unveils every aspect of the city via its efficient search engine. You'll find up-to-date lisitings of accommodation, restaurants, shopping, nightlife and attractions.

PRIME TRAVEL SITES

www.fodors.com
A complete travel-planning site. You can research prices and weather; book air tickets, cars and rooms; ask questions (and get answers) from fellow travellers; and find links to other sites.

www.dublinbus.ie
Everything you could possibly need to know about the public bus service, including how to buy the best tickets for your needs. Also information about the DART system and the Luas trams.

INTERNET CAFÉS

Global Internet Café
www.globalcafe.ie
Claims the fastest connection in Ireland.
➕ H6 ✉ 8 Lower O'Connell Street ☎ 878 0295 🕐 Mon–Fri 8–11, Sat 9–11, Sun 10–11 💷 Varies according to time of day

Central Cybercafé
www.globalcafe.ie
Small friendly café. Scanning and CD burning for no extra cost.
➕ H7 ✉ 6 Grafton Street ☎ 677 8298 🕐 Mon–Fri 9am–10pm, Sat–Sun 10–9 💷 Varies according to time of day

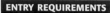

Getting There

ENTRY REQUIREMENTS

For the latest passport and visa information, look up the British embassy website at www.britishembassy.ie or the United States embassy at www.usembassy.ie or call or write to the office (▷ 122).

CUSTOMS

The limits for non-EU visitors are 200 cigarettes or 50 cigars, or 250g of tobacco; 1 litre of spirits (over 22 per-cent) or 2 litres of fortified wine, 2 litres of still wine; 50g of perfume. Travellers under 18 are not entitled to the tobacco and alcohol allowances. The guidelines for EU residents (for personal use) are 800 cigarettes, 200 cigars, 1kg tobacco; 10 litres of spirits (over 22 per cent), 20 litres of aperitifs, 90 litres of wine, of which 60 can be sparkling wine, 110 litres of beer.

AIRPORTS

Dublin Airport is 11km (7 miles) north of the city and has flights to Britain, mainland Europe and North America, as well as to a few other cities in Ireland. Ferries from the UK sail into the ports of Dublin and Dun Laoghaire, 14.5km (9 miles) south of the city.

ARRIVING BY AIR

For information on Dublin Airport ☎ 814 1111. Airlink runs between the airport and the main city bus station only. The journey takes around 20–30 minutes and costs €5. An alternative is Aircoach, costing €7, which makes several stops and runs every 15 minutes 5am–midnight.

The taxi stand is outside the arrivals area. Taxis are always metered, and a journey to central Dublin should cost around €20–€25 (but ask for the price first). Several car rental companies have desks in the arrivals area.

ARRIVING BY BOAT

Ferries from Holyhead sail into the ports of Dublin and Dun Laoghaire throughout the year. The journey takes around 3 hours 15 minutes on a traditional ferry or 1 hour 45 minutes via the high-speed options.

Taxis and buses operate from both ports into the city. The DART light train is easily accessible from Dun Laoghaire, which is 12 km (7.5 miles) from the city hub. When travelling by car from Holyhead terminal, take the N31 to Blackrock. Turn left onto Mount Merrion Avenue and

continue to N11. Turn right and head north to get into town. From Dublin Port take Alexander Road west, turn left at the Point Depot and follow 'city centre' signs.

ARRIVING BY TRAIN
There are two main line stations in Dublin. Passengers from the north of Ireland arrive at Connolly Station, while trains from the south and west operate in and out of Heuston Station. Buses and taxis are available at both stations. Irish Rail is at ☎ 836 6222.

ARRIVING BY CAR
Traffic drives on the left. Congestion in Dublin is increasing, and parking is expensive and limited. It is hoped that the opening of the new Port Tunnel will help aid congestion and keep lorries off the smaller roads. Avoid rush hours, keep out of bus lanes and use designated parking areas. Penalties for illegal parking are severe. Most hotels and guesthouses have parking for guests. Always lock your car and keep belongings out of sight.

INSURANCE
Check your insurance coverage and buy a supplementary policy if needed. EU nationals receive reduced cost medical treatment with an EHIC card. Obtain this card before leaving home. Full health and travel insurance is still advised.

EMBASSIES IN DUBLIN
● Australia
wwwaustralianembassy.ie
● Belgium
www.diplomatie.be/dublin.ie
● France www.ambafrance.ie
● Germany www.germany.ie
● Netherlands
www.netherlandsembassy.ie
● United Kingdom
www.britishembassy.ie
● United States
www.usembassy.ie

For addresses and telephone of the above embassies and consulates, and for information on other countries
(▷ 122).

Getting Around

VISITORS WITH DISABILITIES

Access for wheelchair users has improved in Dublin over recent years. Some public buildings and visitor attractions have ramps and lifts. Those with particularly good facilities are the Guinness Storehouse and the Chester Beatty Library. However, it is always wise to phone in advance. Dublin buses are now incorporating features into some of their buses but routes are still limited so check in advance (☎ 872 0000).

The Irish Wheelchair Association (☎ 818 6400; email: info@iwa.ie) can give advice on accessible accommodations, restaurants and pubs in the city. It can also provide information on wheelchair hire and car hire.

TAXIS

● Useful numbers:
All Sevens Taxi ☎ 677 7777
National Radio Cabs ☎ 677 2222
City Cabs ☎ 872 7272.
See local telephone books for others or ask your hotel to call you a cab.

BUSES

The bus number and destination (in English and Irish) are displayed on the front. An Lar means city centre. Buy tickets on the bus (exact change needed) or before boarding from Dublin Bus office or some newsstands; timetables are also available here. Busáras, the main bus terminus, is north of the River Liffey on Amiens Street.

The DART is a light rail service running from Malahide in the north of the city to Greystones in the south. The main city stations are Connolly (north side) and Pearse (south side). Trains run at least every 5 minutes at peak times, otherwise every 15 minutes Mon–Sat 6.30am–11.30pm and less frequently Sun, 9.30am–11pm. Buy tickets at the station. The Luas is a tram system operating between the suburbs and central Dublin (www.luas.ie). Taxis are in short supply, especially at night. Taxi stands are found outside hotels, train and bus stations, and at locations such as St. Stephen's Green and O'Connell Street.

● Dublin Bus (Bus Átha Cliath) operates Mon–Sat 7am–11.30pm, Sun 10am–11.30pm ☎ 872 0000

● The Nitelink service operates Thu–Sat to the suburbs. Buses leave on the hour from College Street, D'Olier Street, and Westmoreland Street from midnight up until 4.30am; check for individual routes.

● Bus Éireann operates a nationwide coach service that runs from other cities in Ireland ☎ 836 6111

TRAVEL PASSES

● Irish Rail and Dublin Bus sell a range of combined travel passes—single, family, one-day, four-day, weekly (photograph needed). They are not valid for Nitelink, Airlink, ferry services, or tours.

● You can buy all travel passes from Dublin Bus ✉ 55 Upper O'Connell Street. Selected newsstands sell a limited number of passes.

Essential Facts

ELECTRICITY
● 220V AC. Most hotels have 110V shaver outlets.
● Plugs are three square pins.

EMERGENCY PHONE NUMBERS
● Police (garda), fire and ambulance ☎ 999 (free of charge).

ETIQUETTE
● Dubliners are very friendly, so do not be unduly perturbed if strangers strike up conversation. Trust your instincts.
● Do not expect Dubliners to be very punctual. If you are invited to someone's home for dinner, aim to arrive about 10 minutes late.
● Groups of friends and acquaintances usually buy drinks in rounds and if you join them, you will be expected to participate.

GAY AND LESBIAN TRAVELLERS
● *Gay Community News*, a free monthly newspaper, is available from clubs, bars and bookshops.
● Gay and lesbian events in Dublin include the Alternative *Miss Ireland* (March), *Pride* (late June) and the *Lesbian and Gay Film Festival* (late July).
● For information and advice, contact: Gay Switchboard Dublin ☎ 872 1055 ⏰ Mon–Fri 7.30am–9.30pm, Sat 3.30–6pm.

TOURIST INFORMATION
✉ Dublin Airport;
✉ Suffolk Street;
✉ 14 O'Connell Street;
✉ Dun Laoghaire Harbour;
✉ Baggot Street Bridge;
✉ The Square, Tallaght Town Centre
The main tourist office is at Suffolk Street ☎ 605 7700. For information on Dublin visit their website on www.visitdublin.com

OPENING HOURS
Museums and sights: open seven days a week, with shorter hours on Sunday. Call for details.
Shops: six days a week, some seven days; late-night shopping on Thursday. Supermarkets are open longer hours Wed–Fri. Large suburban shopping malls now also stay open Sunday 12–6.
Banks: Mon–Fri 10–4, Thu 10–5.

PLACES OF WORSHIP
Although Ireland is predominantly Catholic, most religious groups have places of worship in Dublin.

Buddhism	Buddhist Centre ✉ 56 Inchicore Road ☎ 453 7427
Church of Ireland	Christ Church Cathedral ✉ Christchurch Place ☎ 677 8099
	St. Patrick's Cathedral ✉ Patrick's Close ☎ 453 9472
	St. Ann's Church ✉ Dawson Street ☎ 676 7727
Methodist	✉ 9c Lower Abbey Street ☎ 874 4668
Muslim	Mosque ✉ 163 South Circular Road ☎ 453 3242
Roman Catholic	St. Mary's Pro-Cathedral ✉ Marlborough Street ☎ 874 5441
	University Church ✉ 87a St. Stephen's Green ☎ 478 0616
	St. Teresa's Church ✉ Clarendon Street, off Grafton Street

NEED TO KNOW ESSENTIAL FACTS

TIPPING

Tips are not expected in cinemas, petrol stations, or in pubs, unless there is table service.

Ten per cent is customary for hairdressers and taxi drivers; porters, doormen and clockroom attendants €2.

See ▷ 85 for restaurant tipping.

MONEY

The euro is the official currency of Ireland. Bank notes in denominations of 5, 10, 20, 50, 100, 200 and 500 euros and coins in denominations of 1, 2, 5, 10, 20 and 50 cents and 1 and 2 euros were introduced on 1 January 2002.

10 euros

50 euros

200 euros

500 euros

Outhouse Gay Community and Resource Centre ✉ 105 Capel Street ☎ 873 4932

MEDICINES AND MEDICAL TREATMENT

● Ambulance ☎ 999 or 112.

● Hospital with 24-hour emergency service: St. Vincent's ✉ Elm Park, Dublin 4 ☎ 221 4000

● Daytime dental facilities: Anne's Lane Dental Centre ✉ 2 St. Anne's Lane ☎ 671 8581. For dental referrals: Irish Dental Association ✉ Leopardstown Office Park, Sandyford, Dublin 18 ☎ 295 0072

● Minor ailments can usually be treated at pharmacies but only a limited range of medication can be dispensed without a prescription.

● Pharmacies open until 10pm: O'Connell Pharmacy ✉ 55 Lower O'Connell Street ☎ 873 0427; City Pharmacy ✉ 14 Dame Street ☎ 670 4523

MONEY MATTERS

● Banks offer better exchange rates than shops, hotels and bureaux de change.

● The bank at Dublin airport has longer opening hours but charges above-average commission.

● Credit cards can be used in most hotels, shops and restaurants and to withdraw cash from ATMs.

● Most large shops, hotels and restaurants accept travellers' cheques accompanied by some form of identification.

NEWSPAPERS AND MAGAZINES

● The daily broadsheets, the *Irish Times* and the *Irish Independent*, are printed in Dublin. The *Evening Herald* is on sale Mon–Fri at midday. The major UK tabloids also produce separate Irish editions.

● International magazines and newspapers are sold in: Easons ✉ 40–2 Lower O'Connell Street and Tuthills ✉ Royal Hibernian Way

● For events and entertainment listings, check out *In Dublin* and the free *Event Guide*.

● *Hot Press* is Ireland's music magazine, *dSide* is read by fashion-conscious kids and *Image* is Ireland's best-selling women's magazine.

POST OFFICES

● The GPO in O'Connell Street (☎ 705 7000) is open Mon–Sat 8–8. Other post offices are generally open Mon–Fri 9–5.30 and certain city branches open on Saturday. Some suburban offices close for an hour at lunchtime.

● Stamps are sold at post offices, some news-stands, hotels and shops. Books of stamps are available from coin-operated machines outside some post offices.

● Postboxes are green.

SENSIBLE PRECAUTIONS

● Dublin is relatively safe but be cautious.

● Pickpockets and bag snatching are prevalent.

● Keep valuables out of sight.

● Watch handbags and wallets in restaurants, hotels, cafés, shops and cinemas. Don't leave handbags on the backs of chairs.

● Make a separate note of all passport, ticket, travellers' cheques and credit card numbers.

● Avoid Phoenix Park. Women should particu-larly avoid Fitzwillian and Merrion squares, and adjoining streets after dark. They are prime pros-titution areas.

● After dark, women should sit downstairs on buses or in a busy car on trains. Take a taxi rather than a late-night bus out to the suburbs.

TELEPHONES

● Public telephones use coins or phone cards (sold in post offices and news dealers).

● Operator ☎ 10; inland directory enquiries ☎ 11850; UK and overseas directory enquiries ☎ 11860

● Avoid calling from hotels where charges are high. Look for public phones on streets, in pubs and shopping malls.

● The following may be used in front of local telephone numbers: freefone ☎ 1800

ORGANIZED SIGHTSEEING

● City tours by bus leave from O'Connell Street. Buy tickets on board or at Dublin Tourism in Suffolk Street.

● The Dublin Literary Pub Crawl visits pubs frequented by literary giants complete with readings. The tour starts from the Duke pub, Duke Street (☎ 670 5602 🕙 Nov–Easter Thu, Fri, Sat 7.30pm, Sun 12, 7.30; Easter–end Oct nightly 7.30, Sun 12, 7.30).

● The Musical Pub Crawl starts from the Oliver St. John Gogarty pub (☎ 475 3313 🕙 Mid-May–late Oct nightly 7.30; Feb–mid-May, Nov Thu, Fri, Sat 7.30).

● Take a sightseeing cruise of the River Liffey and learn about life in Dublin from the Vikings to the latest dockside redevelopment (☎ 473 4082 🕙 Mar–end Nov daily sailings from 11am).

NATIONAL HOLIDAYS

● 1 January, 17 March, Good Friday, Easter Monday, first Monday in May, Whit Monday (first Mon in May/early June), first Monday in August, All Souls' Day (last Mon in October/ 1 November) 25 and 26 December.

● All pubs and most busi-nesses close on Good Friday. Some shops stay open.

LOST PROPERTY

Report loss or theft of a passport to the police immediately. Your embassy or consulate can provide further assistance.

Airport ☎ 814 555
Ferryport ☎ 855 2296
Train ☎ 703 2101 (Heuston),
703 2362 (Connolly)
Dublin Bus ☎ 703 1321
Bus Éireann ☎ 830 2222

STUDENTS

● Dublin is very student-friendly.
● An International Student Identity Card secures discounts in many cinemas, theatres, shops, restaurants and attractions.
● Discounts may be available on travel cards for the bus and DART.

● When calling from the UK dial 00 353. The code for Dublin is 01 (omit the zero when calling from abroad).
● To call the UK from Dublin, dial 00 44.
● When calling from the US dial 011 353. The code for Dublin is 01 (omit the zero when calling from abroad).
● To call the US from Dublin, dial 00 1.

TELEVISION AND RADIO

● Radio Telefís Éireann (RTÉ) is the state broadcasting authority. It has four radio stations and three television channels.
● Its television stations are RTÉ 1 and RTÉ 2 (mainstream) and TG4, the National Irish Language station. TV3 Ireland is independent.

TOILETS

● Dublin is not renowned for the quality or quantity of its public toilets. Most people go to a pub or large store.
● Signs may be in Irish: *mná*: women, *fir*: men.

EMBASSIES	
Australia	✉ Fitzwilton House, Wilton Place, Dublin 2 ☎ 664 5300
Belgium	✉ Shrewsbury Road, Dublin 4 ☎ 205 7100
Canada	✉ St. Stephen's Green, Dublin 2 ☎ 417 4100
France	✉ 36 Ailesbury Road, Dublin 4 ☎ 277 5000
Germany	✉ 31 Trimleston Avenue, Booterstown, County Dublin ☎ 269 3011
Italy	✉ 63 Northumberland Road, Dublin 4 ☎ 660 1744
Netherlands	✉ 160 Merrion Road, Dublin 4 ☎ 269 3444
Spain	✉ 17a Merlyn Park, Sandymount, Dublin 4 ☎ 269 1640
United Kingdom	✉ 29 Merrion Road, Dublin 4 ☎ 205 3700
US	✉ 42 Elgin Road, Ballsbridge, Dublin 4 ☎ 668 8777

Language

Irish is the official first language of the Republic of Ireland with English as the second. Although the Irish language is still alive and studied by all school children, English is the spoken language in Dublin. Irish is rarely spoken, but the language is enjoying a revival and is fashionable among a younger set proud of their cultural traditions. It is an important symbol of national identity. You will come across Irish on signposts, buses, trains and official documents and the news (*an nuacht*) is broadcast *as gaeilge* on television and radio. *Telefis Na Gaeilge* is a dedicated Irish-language channel with English subtitles. The areas known as the Gaeltacht are pockets of the country where Irish is the main tongue and you will find maps and signposts only using the Galic. These areas are mainly on the western side of Ireland and not in the Dublin vicinity where English is the dominant tongue. The Irish language is difficult for the beginner to grasp with words often pronounced quite differently to the way they are written. To complicate things further there are different Irish dialects and spellings in different regions.

SOME IRISH WORDS TO LOOK OUT FOR:

An Lar	City Centre
Baile Átha Cliath	Dublin
Céilí	Dance
Craic	Fun; laughter; good time
Dia dhuit	Hello
Dúnta	Closed
Fáilte	Welcome
Gardaí	Police
Go raibh maith aguth	Thank you
Leitris	toilet
Mná	Ladies
Fir	Gents
Le do thoil	Please
Níl/ní hea	No
Oifig an phoist	Post Office
Oscailte	Open
Slán	Goodbye
Sláinte	Cheers
Tá/sea	Yes

Timeline

BEFORE AD1000

The Celts landed in Ireland in the 4th century BC and their influence remains even today. Their religious rites included complex burial services. Archaeological excavations have produced some magnificent gold pieces and jewellery, some of which can be seen in Dublin's National Museum (▷ 66).

According to legend St. Patrick converted many of Dublin's inhabitants to Christianity in the 5th century AD. In 841 Vikings established a trading station, probably near present-day Kilmainham. The Vikings moved downstream, to the area around Dublin Castle, in the 10th century.

1014 High King Brian Boru defeats the Dublin Vikings.

1172 After Norman barons invade Ireland from Wales, King Henry II gives Dublin to the men of Bristol.

1348–51 The Black Death claims one third of Dublin's inhabitants.

1592 Queen Elizabeth I grants a charter for the founding of Trinity College.

1700s Dublin's population expands from 40,000 to 172,000.

1712 Work starts on Trinity College Library.

1713 Jonathan Swift is appointed Dean of St. Patrick's Cathedral.

1714 Start of the Georgian era, Dublin's great period of classical architecture.

1745 The building of Leinster House (now home of the Irish Parliament) leads to new housing south of the river.

1759 The Guinness Brewery is founded.

1760–1800 Dublin reaches the height of its prosperity.

1782 Irish Parliament secures legislative independence from Britain.

1800 The Act of Union is passed and the Irish Parliament abolishes itself, prefacing a period of urban decline.

1847 Soup kitchens are set up around Dublin during the Great Famine.

1916 The Easter Rising.

1919 First session of Dáil Éireann (the Irish Parliament) in Mansion House.

1922 Civil War is declared. After 718 years in residence, British forces evacuate Dublin Castle.

1963 Visit by President John F. Kennedy.

1979 The Pope says mass in Phoenix Park to more than 1.3 million people.

1991 The inauguration of Ireland's first female president, Mary Robinson.

1998 The Good Friday Agreement sees a lasting cease-fire in Northern Ireland after decades of troubles.

2001 IRA decommissioned in December.

2004 A no-smoking ban is introduced throughout Ireland in enclosed public places.

2006 Waterside restaurants and galleries thrive in the ongoing Docklands development.

EASTER RISING

With the founding of the Gaelic League in 1893 and the Abbey Theatre in 1904, the movement for independence gathered momentum in Ireland. Frustrated republicans capitalized on England's preoccupation with World War I to stage a rising in 1916 and declare an independent Republic in Dublin's General Post Office. It was doomed to failure but the execution of several of the insurrection's leaders made rebels out of many Irish royalists, leading five years later to the creation of an Irish Free State. The Anglo-Irish Treaty was signed in 1921, followed by a Civil War in 1922, lasting 22 months. In 1936 the Free State became known as Eire under a new Constitution. The Republic finally became a reality in 1949.

From far left: An early city map; helmets in St. Patrick's Cathedral; Great Courtyard of Dublin Castle; Queen Victoria in Dublin at the end of the 19th century

Index

Dublin's
25 BEST

WRITTEN BY Dr. Peter Harbison and Melanie Morris
ADDITIONAL WRITING Hilary Weston and Jackie Staddon
DESIGN CONCEPT AND DESIGN WORK Kate Harling
INDEXER Marie Lorimer
EDITORIAL MANAGEMENT Apostrophe S Limited
REVIEWING EDITOR Jacinta O'Halloran
SERIES EDITOR Paul Mitchell

© Automobile Association Developments Limited 2007 (registered office: Fanum House, Basing View, Basingstoke, Hampshire RG21 4EA, registered number 1878835).

Published in the United Kingdom by AA Publishing

ISBN 978-1-4000-1759-1

FOURTH EDITION

IMPORTANT TIP
Time inevitably brings changes, so always confirm prices, travel facts, and other perishable information when it matters. Although Fodor's cannot accept responsibility for errors, you can use this guide in the confidence that we have taken every care to ensure its accuracy.

SPECIAL SALES
This book is available for special discounts for bulk purchases for sales promotions or premiums. Special editions, including personalized covers, excerpts of existing books, and corporate imprints, can be created in large quantities for special needs. For more information, write to Special Markets/Premium Sales, 1745 Broadway, MD 6–2, New York, NY 10019 or email specialmarkets@randomhouse.com.

First published 1997
Colour separation by Keenes
Printed and bound by Leo, China
10 9 8 7 6 5 4 3 2 1

A02815
Maps in this title based on Ordnance Survey Ireland Permit No. 8136
© Ordnance Survey Ireland and Government of Ireland
Transport map © Communicarta Ltd, UK

The Automobile Association would like to thank the following photographers, companies and picture libraries for their assistance in the preparation of this book.

Abbreviations for the picture credits are as follows: (t) top; (b) bottom; (l) left; (r) right; (AA) AA World Travel Library.

Inside Front Cover (1) Hugh Lane Gallery; **IFC (2)** AA/S Day; **IFC (3)** AA/S L Day; **IFC (4)** AA/S L Day; **IFC (5)** AA/S J Whitehorne; **IFC (6)** AA/S L Day; **IFC (7)** AA/S J Whitehorne; **IFC (8)** AA/W Voysey; **IFC (9)** AA/S L Day; **IFC (10)** AA/C Coe; **1** AA/C Coe; **2** AA/S Day; **3** AA/S Day; **4t** AA/S Day; **4l** AA; **5t** AA/S Day; **5c** AA/S Whitehorne; **6t** AA/S Day; **6cl** AA/C Coe; **6c** AA; **6cr** AA/M Short; **6bl** AA/S Day; **6bc** AA/S Whitehorne; **6br** AA/S McBride; **7t** AA/S Day; **7cl** AA/L Blake; **7cr** AA/S Day; **7bl** AA/S Day; **7br** AA/S McBride; **8** AA/S Day; **9** AA/S Day; **10t** AA/S Day; **10ctr** AA/S Whitehorne; **10cr** AA/S Day; **10cbr** AA/S Whitehorne; **11t** AA/S Day; **11ctl** AA/S Day; **11cl** AA/S Whitehorne; **11cbl** AA/S Whitehorne; **12** AA/S Day; **13t** AA/S Day; **13ctl** AA/Slidefile; **13cl** AA/C Coe; **13cbl** AA/Slidefile; **13bl** AA/C Coe; **14t** AA/S Day; **14ctr** AA/S McBride; **14cr** AA/S Day; **14cbr** AA/S Whitehorne; **14br** AA/S Whitehorne; **15** AA/S Day; **16t** AA/S Day; **16tr** AA/S Whitehorne; **16cr** Photodisc; **16br** AA/D Henley; **17t** AA/S Day; **17tl** AA/M Short; **17ctl** Photodisc; **17cbl** AA/M Short; **17bl** AA/M Short; **18t** AA/S Day; **18tr** AA/S Day; **18ctr** AA/M Short; **18cbr** AA/Slidefile; **18br** AA/S Day; **19t** Guinness; **19ct** AA/S Day; **19cb** AA/S Day; **19b** AA/S Whitehorne; **20/21** AA/S Day; **24l** AA/S Day; **24c** AA/S Day; **24r** AA/S Day; **25l** AA/S Whitehorne; **25r** AA/Slidefile; **26l** AA/S Day; **26c** AA/S Day; **26r** AA/S Day; **27l** Dublinia; 27r Dublinia; **28l** AA/S Day; **28r** AA/S Day; **28/29** AA; **29t** AA/S Day; **29c** AA/S Day; **29cr** AA/S Day; **30** Guinness; **30/31** Guinness; **32l** AA/S Whitehorne; **32c** AA/S Day; **32r** AA/S Day; **33l** AA/S Day; **33c** AA/Slidefile; **33r** AA/M Short; **34l** AA/C Coe; **34r** AA/C Coe; **35t** AA/Slidefile; **35bl** AA/S Day; **35br** AA/S Whitehorne; **36** AA/S Whitehorne; **37** AA/S Whitehorne; **38** AA/M Short; **39** AA/S Day; **40** AA/T King; **41** AA/Slidefile; **42** AA/S Day; **43** AA/S Whitehorne; **44** ImageState; **45** AA/S Day; **48** AA/S Day; **49l** Hugh Lane Gallery; **49r** AA/Slidefile; **50l** AA/S Day; **50c** AA/M Short; **50r** AA/S Day; **51l** AA/S Day; **51cl** AA/S Day; **51cr** AA/S Day; **51r** AA/S Day; **52** AA/S Whitehorne; **52/53** AA/W Voysey; **54t** AA/Slidefile; **54bl** AA/Slidefile; **54br** AA/Slidefile; **55t** AA/Slidefile; **55bl** AA/S Whitehorne; **55br** AA/S Day; **56** AA/S Whitehorne; **57** AA/S Day; **58** AA/C Coe; **59** AA/M Short; **60t** Digital Vision; **60c** AA/S McBride; **61** AA/S McBride; **64l** AA/M Short; **64r** AA/S Whitehorne; **65l** AA/Slidefile; **65c** AA/W Voysey; **65r** AA/S Whitehorne; **66** AA/S Whitehorne; **66/67** AA/S Day; **68l** AA; **68r** AA/M Short; **69l** AA/S Whitehorne; **69r** AA/S Whitehorne; **70tl** AA/S Whitehorne; **70cl** AA/S Day; **70r** AA/S Whitehorne; **71t** AA/S Day; **71cr** AA/S Day; **72t** AA/S McBride; **72cl** AA/S Day; **72c** AA/S Day; **72/73** AA/S McBride; **74t** AA/Slidefile; **74bl** AA/M Short; **74br** AA/S Whitehorne; **75t** AA/Slidefile; **75bl** AA/S Whitehorne; **75br** AA/Slidefile; **76t** AA/Slidefile; **76bl** AA/S Day; **76br** AA/S Day; **77** AA/S Whitehorne; **78** AA/S Whitehorne; **79** AA/S Day; **80** AA/M Short; **81** AA/S Whitehorne; **82t** AA/M Short; **83** AA/C Coe; **84** AA/S Whitehorne; **85** AA/S Day; **86** AA/S Day; **87** ImageState; **88** AA/S Day; **89** AA/C Jones; **92l** AA/S Whitehorne; **92r** AA/S Whitehorne; **93l** AA/S Day; **93r** AA/S Day; **94t** AA/S McBride; **94c** AA/S Whitehorne; **94/95** AA/S Whitehorne; **96l** Irish Museum of Modern Art; **96c** Irish Museum of Modern Art; **96r** Irish Museum of Modern Art; **97t** AA/Slidefile; **97bl** AA/S Whitehorne; **97br** AA/S Whitehorne; **98t** AA/Slidefile; **98b** AA; **99** AA/M Short; **100t** AA/M Short; **100cl** AA/M Short; **100cr** AA/M Short; **100br** AA/C Jones; **101t** AA/M Short; **101bl** AA/S Whitehorne; **101br** AA/Slidefile; **102t** AA/C Jones; **102bl** AA/C Jones; **102br** AA/C Jones; **103t** AA/C Jones; **103bl** AA/Slidefile; **103bc** AA/M Short; **103br** AA/M Short; **104t** AA; **104c** AA/Slidefile; **105** AA/S McBride; **106** ImageState; **107** AA/C Sawyer; **108t** AA/C Sawyer; **108ctr** AA/W Voysey; **108cr** AA/C Sawyer; **108cbr** AA/M Short; **109** AA/C Sawyer; **110** AA/C Sawyer; **111** AA/C Sawyer; **112** AA/C Sawyer; **113** AA/S Day; **114** AA/M Short; **115** AA/M Short; **116** AA/M Short; **117t** AA/M Short; **117c** AA/C Jones; **117b** AA/M Short; **118** AA/M Short; **119** AA/M Short; **120** AA/M Short; **121** AA/M Short; **122t** AA/M Short; **122l** AA/C Jones; **123t** AA/M Short; **123b** AA/S Day; **124t** AA/M Short; **124bl** AA; **124bc** AA/S Day; **124/125** AA; **125t** AA/M Short; **125br** AA.

Every effort has been made to trace the copyright holders, and we apologise in advance for any accidental errors. We would be happy to apply the corrections in the following edition of this publication.